PRAISE FOR
LEAD VERTICALLY

Lead Vertically goes straight to the heart of leadership: others before self, people before mission, and God above all. Craig brilliantly unpacks the process of building into people as the gateway to effective teams and the key to a dynamic ministry. Compelling, insightful and rich with ready-to-implement ideas.

Bill Baumgart
President and CEO, KIDMO

Craig Johnson knows how to lead! I've seen firsthand the impact of his philosophy at Lakewood Church, where he is creating a culture of intentional families, passionate volunteers and effective staff. I encourage every leader to glean inspiration from his vision and to learn from his experience.

Kurt Bruner
Executive Director, The Strong Families Innovation Alliance
Author of *It Starts At Home*

I am thrilled that this book, *Lead Vertically,* has ended up in your hands. Craig is an exceptional leader, and he understands that the greatest way to build our lives is by helping to build the lives of others. This book will inspire you to dream and lead from God's perspective and will equip you with the tools to do it.

Christine Caine
Author of *Stop Acting Like a Christian, Just Be One*

I've seen the way Craig Johnson leads, and I can honestly say that he's living out exactly what he's written! I am so impressed with his level of humility, wisdom and creativity in leading teams. Reading this book will help you learn how to really inspire people in your church to volunteer for the long term.

Amy Dolan
Children's Ministry Leader and Founder of Lemon Lime Kids

Craig Johnson's leadership impacts Lakewood Church every day in the teams he's built, in the staff he oversees, and in the growth it has brought. The proven principles Craig outlines in *Lead Vertically* will give you a look at leadership at a whole new level. Through this book, you will experience hope, encouragement, good stories and practical insights and will be inspired as you enlarge your own vision of leadership from God's perspective!

Dr. Paul Osteen
Associate Pastor, Lakewood Church
Houston, Texas

If you are in the wings waiting for God to place you in a leadership role, put down whatever else you are reading and read this book! Craig has done a masterful job of getting down to the basics of Christian leadership by laying the bedrock of what it takes to be a great leader in the eyes of God. Great leaders—vertical leaders—are those who understand their position in Christ and through His guidance humbly help others do the same. Don't waste another minute . . . take the principles in this book, put them into practice, and let God take your leadership to places you never thought imaginable.

Mike Johnson
Executive producer of *Elevate* and *Elevate Family Curriculum*
Director of FCKids, Fellowship Church
Grapevine, Texas

Craig Johnson is uniquely qualified to write on vertical leadership for one primary reason: he has lived his life and led others from the perspective of heaven. This is needed now more than ever. During times of economic troubles and global dangers when many experts are talking about a "slow and painful recovery" and redefining success as "lowered expectations," Craig reminds us that the most important question to ask is, "How does God see me and my situation?" Both as his pastor and his friend, I have witnessed firsthand how God uses Craig to encourage and inspire leaders and growing believers to throw off limitations and fulfill their divine destiny. Through this book, I believe He will do the same for you.

Dr. Jim Reeve
Senior Pastor, Faith Community Church
West Covina, California

Craig Johnson is an inspirational leader. Those of us who have the privilege of working close to him can testify to his unique ability to motivate and inspire people to follow the vision he articulates. This book is a wonderful tool for all who read it. You will find the help you need to become a better leader.

Marcos Witt
Composer, Singer, and Author
Spanish Pastor, Lakewood Church
Houston, Texas

How do we as Christian leaders mark success? Is it by achieving fancy programming or getting through intense to-do lists? Is it by making grand profits at any cost? In *Lead Vertically*, Craig Johnson refocuses a leader's values and vision . . . ultimately bringing everything back to the truth about success, what it means, what it takes, and how to implement these heart ideas through your team. Be inspired as you read.

Darlene Zschech
Worship Pastor, Hillsong Church
Sydney, Australia

LEAD VERTICALLY

LEAD VERTICALLY

INSPIRE PEOPLE TO VOLUNTEER

BUILD GREAT TEAMS THAT LAST

CRAIG JOHNSON

EDITED BY TOM STEPHEN AND VIRGINIA STARKEY

Regal

From Gospel Light
Ventura, California, U.S.A.

Published by Regal
From Gospel Light
Ventura, California, U.S.A.
www.regalbooks.com
Printed in the U.S.A.

Library of Congress Cataloging-in-Publication Data
Lead vertically : inspire people to volunteer and build great teams that last /
Craig Johnson.
p. cm.
Includes bibliographical references.
ISBN 978-0-8307-5215-7 (hard cover)
1. Christian leadership. I. Title.
BV652.1.J637 2010
253—dc22
2009049211

1 2 3 4 5 6 7 8 9 10 / 15 14 13 12 11 10

Rights for publishing this book outside the U.S.A. or in non-English languages are
administered by Gospel Light Worldwide, an international not-for-profit ministry.
For additional information, please visit www.glww.org, email info@glww.org, or write to
Gospel Light Worldwide, 1957 Eastman Avenue, Ventura, CA 93003, U.S.A.

To order copies of this book and other Regal products in bulk quantities,
please contact us at 1-800-446-7735.

Thank you to Samantha, Cory, Courtney and Connor,
who are God's masterpiece placed in the center of my life.
I love you. Keep Dreaming BIG!

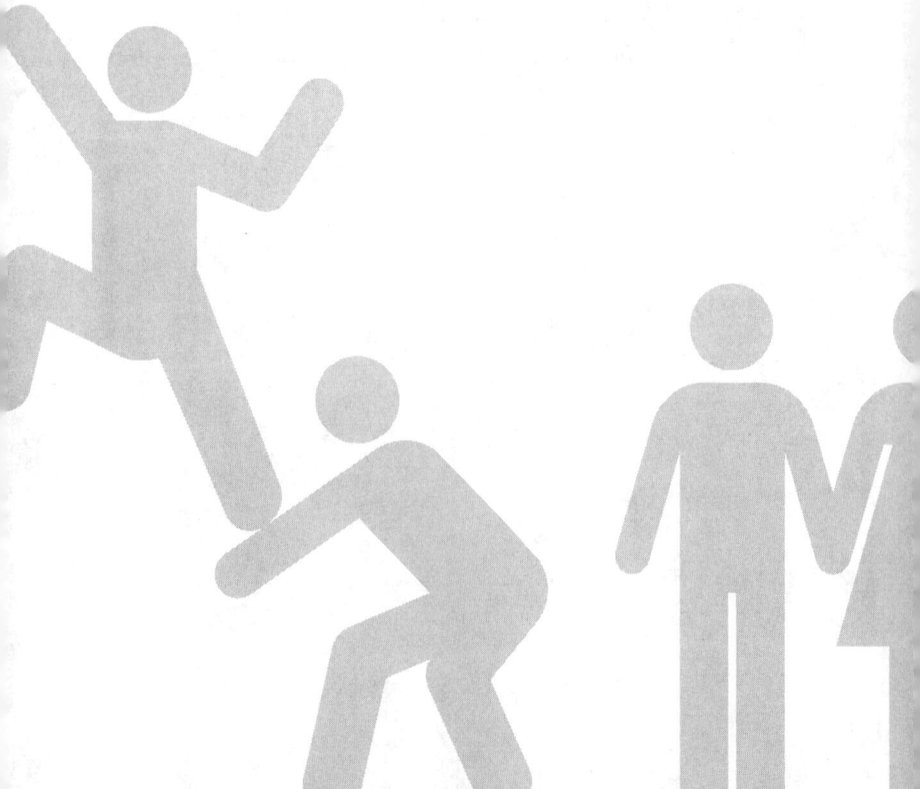

CONTENTS

FOREWORD

Many times God puts big dreams in our hearts, only to see our accomplishments limited because of our small thinking and low expectations. In order to remove those limits and get to that next level in life, we need a new way of thinking, a new perspective. If we want to lead effective lives and effective ministries, we have to lead from God's perspective.

This is just what David wanted when he prayed, "[Lord], Lead me to the Rock that is higher than I" (Psalm 61:2). What was David asking for? David was asking God to give him a new perspective, to take him higher so he could see things from God's perspective.

This higher-level approach to leading and team building is just what Craig Johnson describes in his new book *Lead Vertically*. In it, he will show you how to partner with God to take your ministry, business and family higher, and give you God's perspective on how to grow your organization, how to expand your team and, most importantly, how to build people God's way with dreams, inspiration and hope.

I've seen firsthand how the principles Craig describes in *Lead Vertically* work here at Lakewood Church. A few months before we moved into our new facility (the former Compaq Center), Craig was able to increase our Kidslife volunteer base from 300 to 1,000. The weekend we moved into our new home, our congregation grew from 28,000 to more than 38,000. Had it not been for the accomplishments of Craig and the team he had assembled those few months before the move, Lakewood would not have been ready for the additional 1,500 children that poured into our Kidslife facilities that day. Today, Kidslife continues to minister to more than 4,000 children each week and is a program of which I am proud. Craig's role has now expanded to build several of our other ministry leadership teams as Lakewood's Director of Ministries, using the principles he describes in this book.

I've worked closely with Craig over the last several years and have seen his leadership bring Lakewood Church's Family Ministries to a whole new level. He is a valuable member of our staff and a good friend. We both agree that if you lead vertically, God will take your life and your ministry to a whole new level.

Joel Osteen
Pastor, Lakewood Church

PREFACE

Emily dreamed of serving as a peace officer just like her father. As a child she had played cops and robbers with her two brothers, but she always ended up being the robber because she couldn't make it over the wall on the obstacle course they built.

Their father had taken them to visit the police academy and had told them that the wall was the final obstacle a new officer had to overcome. They built a mini obstacle course at the house and her brothers decided that whoever could get over the wall could be a cop and whoever could not get over the wall would be the robber. Emily would speed through the tires, jump over the mud puddle, and crawl through the plastic tube; but even on a good day she could only get three quarters of the way up the wall. She would fall to the ground with her brothers, yelling, "You're the robber . . . again." Year after year she tried to climb the wall with no success—never the cop, always the robber.

Gradually that mindset seeped into everything she did. She began to feel that she was a loser, not a champion. After high school graduation when her dad encouraged her to apply for the police academy, she was worried. The academic test would be easy for her, but Emily feared the obstacle course. Two instructors were assigned to the cadets to prepare them for the physical test. One instructor worked Emily hard to help her live up to the standards set by her father and brothers. The other instructor didn't say much but kept an eye on everyone and offered encouragement when necessary.

The day of her first attempt, the first instructor berated her, saying, "I heard you can't make it over the wall. Why don't you just go home?" Deep inside she knew he was right. Her attitude determined her actions, and she hit the ground hard, failing to clear the wall. When the first instructor turned away in disgust, the second tried to stop Emily from giving up, saying, "Where are you going, recruit?"

"I'm done," she said. "I'll never be the cop, just the robber."

"Who told you that?" asked the instructor.

"It's a long story," Emily said. "I'm leaving."

"Wait a minute, here's what I want you to do," he said. "I want you to close your eyes and imagine helping someone else climb the wall."

"What? Don't you want me to picture myself climbing the wall?" Emily responded with surprise.

"No," he said, "I need you at the bottom of the wall looking up and believing for someone else. Your struggle isn't just about you; it's about all of the recruits that you will encourage with your story of getting over that wall . . . and you will get over that wall!" he said firmly.

"But I haven't climbed the wall yet; how can I help someone else?"

"When you start building others, God will build you," he replied.

Emily met Ellen the same day she considered quitting the academy. Ellen also found the wall to be an impossible obstacle. With a childlike spirit and the will of a warrior, Emily stopped focusing on herself and started helping Ellen, giving her the encouragement she needed to finally make it over. With arms raised, Ellen yelled, "Yes, we did it!"

"You mean *you* did it," said Emily, joyfully.

"No, *we* did it, and now it's your turn."

For the first time in her life Emily believed she could master the wall. She prayed, "God, if You help me climb this wall, I'll try to always focus on others first, because if I do that, I know You will take care of me."

Emily ran to the wall, grabbed the rope and with her teammate cheering her on, ran up the wall and leapt over. With her hands lifted high in exhilaration, she learned the most important lesson in leadership: Building others ultimately builds you.

Emily's experience as a child had shaped in her an attitude of failure: always a robber, never a cop. She let others dictate her mindset. We all face a similar challenge: Will we let others determine who we are, or will we pursue the purpose for which we were created? If you don't know who you are, someone will tell you who he or she thinks you should be.

Changing one's mindset is a challenge, but it's one of the first obstacles faced by most leaders. Whether you serve on a team or lead the team, you come with attitudes that can prevent you from becoming the person God wants you to be.

Vertical leaders view the world from a different perspective. While they use conventional leadership tools, their primary concern is to see things from God's perspective and help others discover what they were created to do. If you've ever wished you could help your ministry or organization thrive, but your heart has deflated and your mind is confused, then you are ready to see the world differently. You are ready to become a vertical leader. Why? Because you are now at the place where God can use you, because your desperation is birthing God's inspiration. You've stopped seeing things from everybody else's perspective and now see things from God's perspective.

I tell my leaders that when you lose your mind, you should borrow God's. We are not searching for the mind of leadership; we are searching for the mind of God. Vertical leaders have little interest in how others view a situation, but they care how God thinks about it. To achieve success, one has to think unconventionally and believe for the impossible to become possible. Becoming a vertical leader starts with looking up and having the mind of God. What would God say here? How would God build this person? How would God respond in this situation?

Emily expected the instructor to tell her to picture herself climbing over the wall. Instead he told her to help someone else climb the wall. It wasn't a role rehearsal but a mind reversal. When I focus on helping others, I help myself achieve the original goal. Vertical thinking elevates from the bottom to the top. Great mountains are moved not because it's logical but because someone chose to believe. "God Ideas" defy logic and position you to do what nobody else would have even considered.

Recently, I heard a story about our pastor at Lakewood Church, Joel Osteen. A musician was scheduled to sing in the morning worship service and lead worship that evening. After the agreement was made, the musician wanted more time in the service to perform, saying that if he did not get more time, he would not sing. Due to the tight schedule of the service, our worship leadership team denied the artist's request. On Sunday morning, he failed to show up but came strolling down the aisle at the evening service and sat down next to Pastor Joel as though nothing had happened.

Following the service, one of the leaders asked Pastor Joel what to do. Should they only pay him for the service at which he sang? Joel took a piece of paper and wrote down double the amount the guest was originally going to be paid. Why pay him double? The logical thing would have been to pay the guest what he realistically deserved. But Pastor Joel doesn't worry about how others treat him. He's more concerned about how he treats others. Joel knew that God would vindicate him for doing the right thing in the wrong situation. Pastor Joel demonstrated to his entire ministry staff that we are called to think differently and see the world from God's perspective.

Most people think that building a team starts with training leaders to do the program, but building a team starts with training leaders to have the mind of God. Vertical leaders shift their mindset away from feelings and conventional thinking and toward faith-led leadership. They stop relying on their own ideas and start releasing God Ideas. God Ideas are free of the constraints of what our life experiences have led us to believe. Our voice might be able to reach a village, but God's voice can shake a nation.

Vertical leadership calls us to speak with the vocal chords of the God of the universe. "I can do all things through Christ who strengthens me. I am more than a conqueror; I am the head and not the tail; I am blessed and cannot be cursed; I am the cop and not the robber." If you want to build teams, your attitude must match your altitude. If you believe you're always going to struggle, you will always struggle. If you are content with where you are, you will stay there. If you only put half in, you will only get half back.

The greatest lesson I have learned at Lakewood is that there is nothing conventional about God. He can take a church that began in a feed store, and 50 years later move it to an arena. He will give you the dream to build the business and the team to make it happen. Do you have the mind of Christ to do amazing things? Do you elevate your team by inspiring them with what inspires God? Do you limit yourself with leadership ideas, or defy logic with God Ideas? Start with your own thinking before you challenge others to change theirs. If you believe God can help you build great teams and inspire people, you will.

It is my hope that as you read this book, you'll begin to see your ministry or your organization from a new perspective. You'll discover that the key to success does not lie in a paradigm of leadership or a set of skills, but rather it lies in the way you view the world and those you've been given to empower. How do you gain that perspective? How do you become a vertical leader? How do you help others see themselves going over the wall? I'm glad you asked . . .

1

Building the Vertical Leader

*Keep looking up! You never know when God is going
to drop something amazing in your lap.*

Jason's friend was different from the other kids on the block. He rarely came out to play, and when he did, instead of joining in the basketball game, he ran in circles, jumping up and down. His parents watched, hoping their son would connect with the group, only to see that the other children really didn't understand him at all.

When Jason asked his dad why his friend was so different, his father told him about autism, which makes it hard for some kids to communicate and form relationships. Jason was puzzled, and said, "I don't get it."

"Well," his dad replied, "do you ever try to talk to your friend, and he doesn't pay attention?"

"Yes," Jason said.

"Well, that's because he hasn't figured out how to communicate with you. Has he ever repeated things you were saying?"

"Yeah," Jason said, "I thought he was making fun of me."

"No, he is parroting you, trying to figure out how to talk to you."

"Is there a cure for autism?" Jason asked.

"Not yet, but I'm sure people are trying to find one."

Just then, Jason noticed his friend's parents take their son back inside because the other kids were laughing at him. Jason decided right then to help his friend in any way that he could. "Could I find a cure, Daddy?" he said.

Surprised, his dad replied, "Well, it's like I always tell you: keep looking up, because you never know when God is going to drop something amazing in your lap." A big smile came across Jason's face as he realized that anything is possible with God.

Jason collected newspapers and aluminum cans to recycle for profit, and he set up a lemonade stand. When his friends said that he would never make enough money, he just kept looking up. With his parents' help, he planned a walkathon and went door to door asking for donations and telling others of his dream to find a cure for autism. When a door closed without a donation he just kept looking up.

On the day of the walkathon, there were only 10 people signed up to walk (and half of them were his family), but Jason walked proudly around the block, confident that he was making a difference. When a man asked him why he was looking up, Jason told him that God was going to drop something in his lap.

"Right now?" the man replied.

"I don't know," Jason said, "but you'd better duck, just in case!" He was on a mission, and he knew that God was going to come through.

Jason called his family and neighbors and even the local news stations over to hear the announcement of the money he had raised. He was so excited that he woke up at 6:00 A.M. and checked every 15 minutes to see if people were lining up to experience the miracle.

At 9:55, he ran outside to find his mom and dad, a few neighbors, some kids who wanted to see if he actually raised any money, and a local radio station that thought it would make a cute story for their lifestyles segment. Jason began to speak: "Ladies and gentleman, members of the press, thank you for coming out today to help find the cure for autism. The money we raised will help my friend be cured so that he can play basketball whenever he wants to. Let the change begin!"

At that moment, Jason unscrewed the back of his piggy bank and poured out the money he had raised during the past three months. As his mom and dad counted the money, he began to wonder why his friend with autism had not shown up. Then Jason's dad called out, "$435." With great confidence Jason shouted, "YES! We have done it!" In his mind, $435 was the equivalent to $4,000,000. Kids started laughing, saying, "$435 wouldn't cure a frog." A neighbor gave him a pat on the head, saying, "You did your best, son; that's all you can do."

For the first time in three months, Jason dropped his head in embarrassment. "I did my best, Daddy," he said. "I guess it just wasn't good enough." His father smiled and said, "Son, when you give your little, God will take care of the rest. Keep your head up; you never know when God is going to drop something amazing in your lap."

Later that day, Jason's friend and his parents returned home. Jason ran over to knock on their door and ask why they had missed the big announcement about the money he raised. The parents explained that they had been visiting a developmental school that could help their son, but were discouraged because the school cost $35,936 per year. "There's no way we can afford a school like that."

Jason replied, "Guess what? I raised $435 for your son, so we only have a little over $35,000 more to go." They thanked him, but were still discouraged, so Jason said the only thing he knew to say: "Keep your head up. You never know when God may drop something amazing in your lap."

Just then, Jason's dad came in with an envelope, which he dropped into the parents' laps. "A courier just delivered this to our house," he said. The couple opened the envelope and began to read the note:

We just heard on the radio about the little boy who wants to find a cure for his autistic friend. Our son was born with autism years ago, and at the time there was very little known about how to help him. We have always wished we could do for someone else what we couldn't do for our son. We recently sold some property, and when we heard about Jason's desire to help his friend, we knew we were meant to help in some way. Enclosed is a check for the amount we received in the sale of our property, $430,917. Thank you for letting us help your son.

The parents began to dance around with their little boy. Pulling his calculator out, the father confirmed that the check would pay for 12 years of school.

No one can foresee all the obstacles he or she will face personally, in business or in ministry. It wasn't a lack of challenges, but rather his response to them that helped Jason succeed. In other words, his response determined his experience of providence. He experienced God's best because he saw the world from God's perspective: He kept looking up.

This story (based loosely on the actual event of my family receiving a tremendous gift for my son with autism) demonstrates the basic principle behind vertical leadership:

> *A vertical leader sees life on a different plane and inspires extraordinary change that helps others soar above their circumstances.*

Leadership from God's Perspective

At a recent visit from a youth group at Lakewood Church, one of our team leaders, Clayton Hurst, embodied vertical leadership when he met Alex and Savannah. He remembered teaching Savannah as a toddler, when she had been a bright, confident little girl. As she grew she excelled in everything she did. But Savannah took after her parents physically, having inherited her mother's red hair and her parents' height.

Not having seen her since she was a young girl, Clayton was surprised at how tall both she and her brother were. Though only a sophomore, Alex was already six foot six. "Alex, you are huge!" shouted Clayton. Alex put his head down, shy but loving being seen as a man. He told Clayton proudly about having lettered in three sports as a sophomore. When Savannah came around the corner, Clayton saw that she, too, was very tall for her age, and he held his arms open and said, "Savannah, you are so beautiful!" A big smile flashed across her face and she talked to him for a few minutes about how she was doing.

Clayton had no idea that his vertical leadership had had an impact on Savannah. He received the following email from her mother the next day:

> I'm sure you didn't know this, but Savannah's been going through an awkward time right now because of her height. Both the girls and boys in her grade are shorter than she is, and events like dances have been miserable! One girl told her she was a freak. When most people see her, they say, "Oh my gosh, you are huge!" "Huge" isn't what a young girl wants to hear. When you saw her and said, "You are so beautiful," it meant the world to her. It opened the door to a good conversation with her and I know it blessed her. It was a small seed of confidence. My heart is full of gratitude for the way God's love shows through your actions.

In seeing Savannah as beautiful, and not just tall, Clayton lifted her spirits and her confidence. Vertical leaders help others soar where eagles fly, not where the chickens grovel. They realize that power is not attained by climbing a corporate ladder but through the building of people. Savannah's mom now views Clayton as an outstanding leader, not because of some program but rather because of what he saw in her daughter. Vertical leaders see building others as the best way to experience God's work in their own life. Savannah needed to see her world from a new perspective, and Clayton inspired her to do just that.

It's Not Always Obvious

God's vertical leaders are not always the obvious choice. The great leaders that God uses are not always stereotypical, but they are available. In his book *A Tale of Three Kings,* Gene Edwards describes Saul being chosen as king because he fit the image of a king.[1] He was tall, good looking and well liked. He came from a good lineage and did great things for his people. Yet, despite the image, Saul's jealousy and self-importance were eventually revealed. His pride prevented him from becoming everything God intended for his life. Instead of a favored king, he became what Gene Edwards calls a mad king.

David, on the other hand, displayed few of the characteristics of leadership. Like Saul, David's brothers fit the image of a leader, while David was merely a lowly shepherd boy. If David and Saul were running for the office of king, Saul would have won. Yet, who we think should be king may not be who God thinks should be king. God sees the character and potential in a person. While caring for sheep, seeds of leadership were planted in David. Eventually he rose above his circumstances to become one of the greatest kings in history. He learned that everyone was important, that with God's help he could defeat his enemies, and that strength and power have nothing to do with the size of a person's body, but everything to do with the size of his or her heart. In other words, big doors swing on little hinges.

When you have the mind of God, you do not simply pursue people that everyone else notices. We pursue those who others never notice. You never know what you might find until you draw it out of them. Your David may be sitting where no one is looking.

Vertical Leaders Are Shaped Through Experience

As a vertical leader, God has uniquely gifted you with particular strengths. He has also given you experiences that have shaped you. True inspiration comes from divine collaboration. When God directs your life, He inspires the words and orchestrates the music. Your best songs are yet to be written. Life can be like writing a song. The melody and lyrics you play will depend on who is composing. Will you allow God to lead while you play? He'll use your life to inspire others to really live. Remember, if you speak from your mind, you will reach a mind; if you speak from your heart, you will reach a heart; if you speak from your life, you will reach a life.

Most leadership lessons come from experiences at a pivotal point in your life or a difficult circumstance in which you needed to find a solution. Vertical leaders learn more from their experiences than from generic leadership principles. When David defended the sheep against the lion and bear, he learned the art of warfare that would help him defeat Goliath. When he wrote praises to God in the fields, he learned humility and thanksgiving. David could not have known that those songs would become a prayer book, but God knew. God thinks ahead and prepares us to inspire others.

The more you pursue growth, the more you learn. When you take time to reflect and learn from both the good and the bad experiences in your life, you will grow as a leader.

When the doctor diagnosed our son Connor with autism, we were shocked. My wife and I had very little knowledge of autism and what it would mean for our family. As you'll see throughout this book, our experience with autism and God's provision have helped us see life on a totally different plane. We've walked through difficult and heart-breaking moments, but what I've learned as I've watched Connor grow is that he has the heart of a champion. Like him, we can never give up.

Upon his diagnosis, we experienced the fear and trauma of not understanding why God did not immediately heal our son. But even in what appeared to be God's lack of response, we still believed that God was working. Victoria Osteen says, "God's silence is not God's denial. He is constantly working behind the scenes on our behalf." Our struggle has helped us identify with other families, in similar situations, that need to support their children. I've sensed God's call to lead others in developing a ministry at our church to help families develop their children. When we looked up, we saw God's desire to create a place for children to grow and learn.

Everyone has had experiences that God wants to use to shape their leadership. If you were to record 10 examples in which someone or something impacted you, what principles of leadership would begin to form in your mind? You would probably be able to write a book! Our life is like a book: What you choose to do with your life dictates whether it's an adventure or blank pages.

Vertical leaders take those principles learned and put a constant stream of upward thoughts into motion. Perspective is changed when you see life from a different viewpoint. You understand that each experience you've been given can inspire others toward extraordinary change.

A Google Earth Lens

The website Google Earth displays images allowing users to look down on the earth from a bird's-eye view. A satellite shows what the human eye could never see. When I allow God to be my satel-lite, I am able to rise above what I can't understand but God can. What I can't move, God can. What I can't resolve, God can. What I can't see, God can.

When we are assured that God is working things together for our good—when we trust in His ability to work in even the most difficult situations—problems look like molehills instead of mountains. Why? Imagine placing a problem in your hand and looking at it from every angle with a magnifying glass. Vertical leaders can see the world from that perspective when they look through God's lens.

A vertical leader always looks up. If you cast your head down, you will not be able to see what's ahead. If you look forward, you can only see what's in front of you. But if you always look up, you'll see that God has everything under control. It's the Google Earth perspective.

When David faced off in battle against Goliath, he spoke with the confidence of a vertical leader. He said, "You come against me with a sword and spear and javelin, but I come against you in the name of the LORD Almighty, the God of the armies of Israel, whom you have defied. This day the LORD will hand you over to me" (1 Sam. 17:45-46). David saw his victory long before it happened, be-cause he saw the world from a different perspective. It's interesting that God told David to pick five smooth stones. Why not just pick up one stone? Maybe because the other four stones were symbolic of what David was going to use in the battles to come. God had given him the tools of faith before he ever got to the fights yet to come; God knew what lay ahead.

In chess, the player who sees the big picture can see every move before it's made; Grandmaster Champions not only see their own moves, but they can also see every move their opponent will make. At that point, victory is inevitable. What a difference it would make to work from what God knows and what He can see. Spiritually we can have the mind of God and see things through His eyes.

Are you ready to see life from God's perspective? Are you ready to inspire and be inspired by others? Are you ready to develop a heart attitude that will inspire extraordinary change in the teams that you lead? It all begins as you begin to incorporate two key characteristics of Vertical Leadership: the heart of a child and the will of a warrior.

Looking Up from the Trenches

Margaret Perez
Lakewood Volunteer

During my year as an intern, Pastor Craig has had a major influence on me by shaping the kind of leader I want to be. It is so easy for a person's past to determine his or her future. We allow the circumstances surrounding us to shape who we are and how we relate to others. We forget that we were created in God's image, not the image of who people think we should be. The true motives in our heart will always show, our true character will eventually be known and the seed planted in our inner person should be of God's heart—God's image.

During conversations with Pastor Craig, we talked about the choices that we all make: We can make the popular choice or we can make the right choice, by looking up, for God's perspective. Leaders with position and power can sometimes lose sight of their true objective and the reason why they were placed in leadership.

By thinking vertically rather than looking at what is right in front of me, I have learned that it is not all about me! As leaders, we forget that one word, one song, one touch or even one prayer can make a difference in a person's life. I know that through God's leadership, I want to be a reflection of His path and invite others on His road.

At the beginning of my children's ministry internship, I struggled with becoming who God has called me to be. Pastor Craig saw my heart for children's ministry and God's calling, even before I knew it was there. At times I would ask Pastor Craig, "Does it get any easier?" The answer came back, "No, it doesn't get easier, but God makes you stronger and makes your heart bigger. The harder it gets the more you look up." By looking up, you get God's perspective and begin to grow in confidence. Your vision does not become one of the natural but of the supernatural. God gives you just enough.

I have learned that when you are in search for God's guidance, troubles may shake you and people may strike you, but all the pressures of life just bring out the love of God with which you are filled. Through Pastor Craig's example, I have learned to be an encourager to others and even to myself. As a leader, I have learned that when we sow seeds of hope, faith and encouragement into the lives of those around us, God will bring people into our lives to encourage us. When God's passion is in your heart, it will radiate and become contagious to others around you.

At a leaders meeting for a brand-new church, the pastor said to his leaders, "Just imagine when we are running two services a Sunday. Think about how you will feel then." Everyone had an overwhelmed look on his or her face. I spoke up, saying, "We'll be thanking God the whole time, because with God on our side, all things are possible."

When you stop thinking that everything is overwhelming or that everything will fail, you can develop the attitude of possibilities. God stretches us just enough. We are like a rubber band in

God's hands. When first stretched, the rubber band has a little resistance; but the more it's stretched, the less resistance there is. God knows just how much He can stretch us before we break.

Pastor Craig has taught us to always think of ourselves as leaders. You don't have to carry a title in front of your name to be a leader to others around you. As a single parent, I am Mom and Dad to both of my children. Through God's strength, guidance and wisdom, I am able to show them that we can do it. I refuse to allow my "single parent" status and our past to influence their character, determine who they are, or diminish who God has created them to be.

Through Pastor Craig's encouragement, I have learned that when God has called you to step out of the boat, and when God tells you it is time to *go*, you look up and you *go*.

QUESTIONS FOR ACTION

1. Identify the people in your life who fit the definition of a Vertical Leader.

2. As a leader, do you see the best in people? What steps can you take to build into the people you lead?

3. How can the phrase "big doors swing on little hinges" impact your view of identifying leadership qualities in others?

4. Record 10 examples in which someone or something has had an impact on you. What principles of leadership begin to form in your mind?

5. What can you do in the next 30 days to develop a Google Earth perspective?

Note
1. Gene Edwards, *A Tale of Three Kings* (Chicago, IL: Tyndale, 1992).

2

The Heart of a Child and the Will of a Warrior

No great pursuit has ever been accomplished without the undying will of one person willing to carry a cause. These are the people who change the world.

A vertical leader cannot be built from reading a book or attending a leadership conference. Vertical leaders develop the ability to see from God's perspective by developing a heart to listen and the will to do what needs to be done. A vertical leader inspires others to soar above their circumstances by cultivating two birthmarks that identify them as champions of hope: the heart of a child and the will of a warrior. What was unique about Jason wanting to find a cure for autism? His motives were pure and his mind was not shaped by the worries of life. With a mission, and a father to guide him, nothing could hold him back. His father planted a seed in him: to look up and expect God's best. Once Jason received the seed, he began to think vertically, and his iron will almost guaranteed his success. You can't receive the harvest until you accept the seed.

In Matthew 13:22-23, Jesus interprets part of a parable about a man throwing seeds into a field. The seed that fell among thorns represents those who hear God's Word, but the worries of life and the lure of wealth crowd out the message. The seed that fell on good soil represents those who hear and understand God's Word and produce a harvest of 30, 60, or even 100 times greater than what was planted.

Like the man who sowed in the parable, we as vertical leaders plant seeds in those we lead. Will we plant seeds that come from ourselves or will we plant a vision in our team that comes from above? If we nurture it with our own thoughts and knowledge, we put ourselves first. We think we can somehow control the growth of the seed with our own abilities and get better results. We say, "I'll just do it myself," or "What do they know? I've been leading for 20 years; there is nothing new they can teach me," or "You're either for me or against me." If we act on our own, we miss out on the joy of leading with God and with others. Exclusivity won't make you a better leader, just a lonely one. God doesn't do one-man shows; we all need help to produce a great harvest.

I've heard it said that a warrior is not about perfection or victory or invulnerability; he's about absolute vulnerability. Having the heart of a child allows you to admit you need help—from others and from God. It is tempting to seek perfection instead of others' participation. People may admire perfection but they can't relate to it. When you aren't able to admit you are wrong or apologize for a mistake, you become a dangerous leader. We think our image will be damaged because strong leaders do not make mistakes. We feel like our team will think less of us when we fall short. Yet it is our very mistakes that help others connect to us.

Everyone makes mistakes, but not everyone is willing to admit to it. Everyone already knows you aren't perfect, so why put a fortress around the image you want people to believe? You are going to make mistakes. Use them as character-building times to grow yourself and your team. Our character is demonstrated in how we respond to the mistakes we make. We can be invulnerable and build an image, or we can be vulnerable and build a life.

Investing in others' lives takes time, energy and commitment. Sometimes it seems easier to just do it on your own. Yet when you neglect to build other leaders to share the work, the load becomes too heavy. No leader's legs are that strong. How many leaders do you know who've burned out or broken down under the strain of trying to carry the entire weight of the organization? There is tremendous value in including others and building teams. An old leadership joke asks, "What do you call a leader who has no one following him?" Answer: A person on a walk. If you don't have anyone working with you, you are not a leader. A vertical leader is inclusive and builds up whoever is willing to follow.

I love the story of the little boy playing quietly in his backyard while his father watched from the window. The father took great joy in watching his son play with his trucks in the sandbox. As the boy began to dig another tunnel, he hit a rock and got frustrated and started to cry. Although the father wanted to go outside to help, instead he decided to watch and see how his son handled his problem. Quickly the boy's sad face became determined, and he began to dig around the rock. It was too heavy to lift out, so, getting a stick, he tried to pry the rock loose. The stick broke and, frustrated, the boy kicked the rock, hoping it would move. Now his foot hurt, and he began to cry, yelling, "Stupid rock." Throwing his toys down, he ran inside the house where his father met him.

With great disappointment the boy told his father about the rock and everything he had done to try to move it. "I hate that rock, because it's impossible to move!"

"Can you think of anything else you could have done?" the father asked.

With great frustration the boy explained that he had done everything possible to move the rock.

"Son, you could have moved that rock, but you forgot to use your greatest help. Me. Had you called on me, I would have helped you. Always remember that you don't need to do things on your own; when you ask, there will always be someone to help."

Over the years I've been honored to watch countless volunteers help children in their time of need. My son Connor plays in a baseball league for special-needs kids called the Challenger League. Where most kids can pick up a bat and swing it, Connor will let the bat drop to the ground. My daughter, Courtney, volunteered to be Connor's baseball buddy. She showed him how to catch, run, swing the bat and just have fun.

When Connor went up to bat for the first time, we all waited in anticipation for him to get his first hit. Courtney assisted him to the batter's box, helped him get in a stance and wait for the pitch. The first pitch came and Courtney let Connor try to swing on his own, but he dropped the bat. With the second pitch, she got behind Connor and helped him swing and hit the ball. The ball barely moved, but to him it felt like he had knocked it out of the park. It was brilliant watching our daughter help our son get his first hit. What Connor couldn't do on his own, Courtney created the possibility of his success because they did it together. We screamed, "Run, Connor" and instead of going to first base, he took off for center field. What a moment!

Most teenagers would probably prefer to be at the mall hanging out with their friends rather then chasing their little brother in the outfield. Why would a teenager want to mess with a little kid when she could be doing grown-up stuff? She had the heart of a child.

Society will demand that you grow up, but God will require your heart to stay forever young. When the little children ran to Jesus and wanted to climb on His lap, the disciples tried to stop them. Jesus had the heart of a child and told the disciples to let the children come to Him, because the kingdom of God belongs to people who are like these children. He said, "I tell you the truth, anyone who will not receive the kingdom of God like a little child will never enter it" (Mark 10:15). In other words, if you want the keys to the Kingdom, you must have the heart of a child.

Having the will of a warrior is the second identifying mark of a vertical leader. Some would say that humility and a strong will don't go together, but nothing could be further from the truth. When you are willing to listen to God, and your will intertwines with God's will, anything is possible.

My Grandma Surratt faced many challenges in life, but none was greater than cancer. She had a smile, a hug and kiss, and a big meal waiting for me every time I came to visit. I was her boy. She called me Craig-O. If we were going to visit and I tried to place an order over the phone, she would say, "Craig-O, I already know what you want. I will start frying the chicken and cooking the corn. I'll slice up some tomatoes just the way you like them." When I knocked on the door, she would drop what she was doing and rush to greet me. We had a special bond that is hard to explain except by saying I could feel her hugging me from a thousand miles away.

Unfortunately, my grandmother didn't find out about her cancer until it was too late. For seven years she had the will of a warrior and fought through the pain. During those years, for the most part, the only Grandma I saw was upbeat, excited to see me, with a smile on her face and a meal in her kitchen. Then I got the call from my mom saying that Grandma was being rushed to the hospital. The doctor said I probably would not make it in time to say good-bye.

He didn't know my grandmother! She was stubborn, with the will of a warrior. Although cancer had ravaged her body, and every breath was labored, she knew it wasn't time to let go because there was one person who wasn't there yet, her boy, Craig-O. She slipped in and out of consciousness, but every time she woke, she would ask, "Where's my boy?" After being reassured, "He'll be here as soon as he can," she would drift off again.

Before I boarded the plane, my mom said, "She keeps asking for you; she won't let go until you get here. Hurry, Craig." I was worried that I wouldn't make it in time, but I had failed to realize that she had the will of a warrior. When I got off the plane, my mom said, "You won't believe it, she's still fighting." God was honoring her fighting spirit, because God loves the will of a warrior. He kept breathing life into her so her grandson could love on her one last time and let her know it was okay to go.

My sister met me at the hospital, saying, "Craig, it's a miracle she is still alive." She refused to stop fighting until she had finished what she had purposed to do. As I walked into the room, I said, "Grandma, I'm here, your boy is here; I love you." With every bit of strength she had she took a breath and said, "Craig, I love you." Those four words were all she could manage but they were enough for the both of us. She was gone before the next sunrise, but she did what she set out to do. My mother told us that before her final battle in the hospital, she talked about having peace, knowing that she had fought the good fight of faith and that she had finished the race. But she had one more battle to fight. She wanted to make sure her boy had peace too.

What does it take for a person to bounce back, to fight through until his or her last breath? When your will is intertwined with God's will, that is the will of a warrior. John Osteen said, "Great it is to dream the dream when you stand in youth by the starry stream, but GREATER it is to fight life through and say in the end the dream is true."[1] Determination and perseverance to pursue God's purpose, combined with a humble heart, give vertical leaders the ability to see life on a whole different plane.

When you see things from God's perspective, you'll be asked to do things that seem impossible. But as you trust God like a child, ask others for help and develop the will to see God's best come to fruition, no matter what, you'll see your greatest dreams and hopes become a reality. Nothing will stand in the way of living out your purpose.

A Vertical Perspective

When I was considering coming to Lakewood Church, I flew out to meet the staff and experience the church firsthand. As we drove to the church, I couldn't believe how much traffic there was on a Sunday morning. I thought, *Is there a fair or a festival going on around here?* You can imagine my surprise when we realized all these cars were lined up to get into Lakewood Church. I had seen cars lined up on the 57 Freeway, in Anaheim, California, for an Angels' baseball game, but never to go to church!

When we finally made it to the church, I went into the kids' facilities, which while very nice and clean, were unlike the 40,000 square foot, state-of-the-art facility called Kidznet at Faith Community Church in California. At Faith Community, we believed that when someone walked onto our campus and experienced our people and facility, they would know that we valued families and children. Lakewood had a similar vision, but their facilities didn't yet match their vision.

They had outstanding teachers and leaders, but the infrastructure needed to expand to accommodate the increase in children and services that was right around the corner. Worship teams, drama teams, security teams for kids, registration teams, programmers, ministry leaders, sound and tech teams all needed to be built for the expansion of the children's ministry. Multiple levels of leadership development were needed to recruit and train the large number of leaders we were going to need in the future. I remember saying to my wife, "Why do we want to leave California and start over?" We loved our neighborhood, the weather, our church and our new kids' facility. God helped us build the ministry to have a big impact in our church and community.

As I considered Lakewood, I was overwhelmed with the task in front of me, and I accosted my wife with questions: "Do you know how hard this job is going to be? Do you know how many teams we need to build just to handle the number of kids that are going to come? Do you have any idea the vision that Joel Osteen has for this church?"

We went to dinner with Joel and Victoria Osteen, as well as Lisa and Kevin Comas, Joel's sister and brother-in-law, who were leaders at the church. To my surprise, about a quarter of the way through dinner, Joel turned to me and said, "Craig, we want to reach kids and families like we have never done before. We could have moved into the Compaq Center earlier than our projected date, but we wanted to make kids and families a priority. Our facilities are going to be state of the art, but we need a leader that can help take us to that next level. I believe that you are that leader. I believe that with God's help we can have one of the best children's ministries in the country, and we believe you could be with us for the next 25 years."

That was my first experience talking to Joel Osteen. I thought to myself, *Who is this guy?* He is the nicest guy in the world, but he's also one of the most focused people I have ever met. He didn't waste any time getting to the point. In that moment, I saw both the heart of a child and the will of a warrior. He operated on a completely different plane than any other leader in my life. His positive but determined faith inspired me. What leader would actually tell someone they'd just met that he felt he was going to be with him for the next 25 years? What I've discovered is that Joel is one of the most loyal people you will ever meet. If he says he believes you could be with him for 25 years, he is not doing a sales job. He has a childlike faith and belief in people.

After dinner, I told my wife what Joel had said and she laughed, saying, "Was he serious? Twenty five years?" I said, "Yes, I think so." We were both dumbfounded that after one interview he would boldly invite us to spend a good part of our life working with him. That night we both acknowledged that Joel doesn't see things the same way most leaders see things. He didn't pretend to be positive for the sake of appearance; he actually believes everything he says. Children are like that, aren't they? They say what they mean and they mean what they say.

I went to church the next morning and felt torn between being inspired by my new surroundings and not wanting to leave our life and ministry in California. I thought to myself, *Why would God bring us to a place we love for only three years and want us to leave? We were just getting started.* I had a sense that our call to Lakewood was inevitable, but I was not yet ready to give up the fight.

At times we let pride, security, insecurity, stubbornness or fear freeze us in place. I call it cryogenic leadership. We are frozen in our current state of being, holding on to the known because the unknown doesn't make sense. Yet, what has ever happened supernaturally that makes sense? Nothing truly great ever makes sense.

When Nehemiah felt called to rebuild the wall around Jerusalem, it didn't make sense; he was just the cupbearer to the king. When Moses parted the Red Sea by raising his staff, it didn't make sense, yet the sea split in half. When Joshua fought the battle of Jericho by marching around the city seven times, it didn't make sense, yet the walls of Jericho fell down. Your thoughts hold you back more than any enemy ever could. If we try to make sense of everything, we'll reason ourselves out of ever doing anything great for God.

In Lakewood's worship service that morning, Duncan Dodds introduced himself, and the first words out of his mouth were, "If you can dream it, we can help you make it happen." *Who are these people?* I thought. *This is the most positive church I've ever seen and they all speak the same language.* After the service, we met with Paul Osteen, who looked at me and said, "I don't know what you are waiting for; this feels right to me. We believe that you are the right one to come to Lakewood."

Still not feeling a release to leave Faith Community Church, I began mentally packing my bags, because the interviews were over and I was ready to go home. Then Joel called me, saying, "Now, Craig, we don't want to pressure you, but we really feel that you are the right person to be with us at Lakewood. Just know that we are believing with you for God's best for you and your family, although we think God's best is here at Lakewood." He was seeing what God had already confirmed and was just waiting for me to see it too. They didn't necessarily need me. After all, they could have chosen from any number of more talented and qualified people. Yet, vertical leaders don't choose based on human qualifications; they choose those God has already chosen. Vertical leaders are looking up to see God's perspective. Remember, who we think should be king may not be who God thinks should be king.

Just then, I received a phone call from my sister and told her about the amazing time I had had at Lakewood and how nice they all were and how much love I felt being there, but that I just didn't feel a confirmation to leave our home in California.

A pretty straightforward thinker, my sister will usually say what's on her mind. Her first words were, "What is the matter with you? Do you realize the opportunity God is giving you to work with someone like Joel and reach thousands of people through the incredible movement that's taking place there? Do you realize what God has placed you in the middle of?" Feeling the presence of the Holy Spirit surrounding me, I began to cry. My wife, who had only heard my side of the conversation, was sitting on the bed crying because she felt the same confirmation at the same time: We were leaving California and moving to Texas to be a part of Lakewood. What had happened? While I was still letting my feelings and thoughts control my destiny, God was using vertical leaders to help me see things I was unable to see on my own. I was thinking of all the reasons I couldn't come instead of being open to hearing all the reasons we could.

The phrase "vertical leaders" came to me a year before we went to Lakewood. Little did we know that we would be serving with so many vertical leaders who would teach us how to rise above our circumstances in spite of our difficulties. Not only would we have the challenge of building teams and growing a large ministry, but we would also find out that our son Connor had autism. If we were going to fulfill God's destiny in our lives, we would need to have the heart of a child to accept God's plan and the will of a warrior to fight the battles we were about to face.

Are you willing to develop the heart of a child and the will of a warrior? As you read this book, you'll explore both the essence and characteristics of a vertical leader. You'll discover that vertical leadership happens when we focus outwardly, both on God's perspective and on loving others. Jesus once said that the two greatest commandments were to love God and to love others. Great leadership has at its heart the same two commands. I've heard it said that a warrior does not give up in what he loves; he finds the love in what he does.

Looking Up from the Trenches

Falon Moore
Lakewood Volunteer

"Welcome, we are so glad to have you here!" These were the first words spoken to me by Pastor Craig Johnson. I don't know if he could read the apprehension and nervousness on my face, but he succeeded in easing my fears and making me feel welcome. I was completely removed from my element, having just moved from an 800-member suburban church in New Jersey to be an intern at Lakewood, the largest church in America. Intimidated, I wondered if I was capable of the task ahead of me.

Pastor Craig's reputation preceded him. I had heard how he came from California to Lakewood to help build the children's ministry and how he and the staff had built a team of more than 1,000 volunteers. I saw the programs that he and his team had implemented, and how the children's ministry ran like a well-oiled machine. I knew so much about Pastor Craig before I actually met him. As an outsider looking in, one might think he would be untouchable or just too busy. Nothing could be further from the truth.

My first encounter with Pastor Craig was in my intern training class. He took time to show a personal interest in each of us and offer encouragement. Valuing others, remembering "the team" and thinking with the mind of Christ were just a few of the lessons he taught us. He modeled for us how to be vulnerable and how to share in the struggles and triumphs of those around us. He was truthful about life in ministry, always encouraging us to check the heart and motives behind our actions and to never take God's people for granted.

On one occasion, Pastor Craig was teaching our class while in the midst of facing a major decision that would affect many within the church. He didn't pretend that he had it all together or that it wasn't weighing on his heart. He knew that God was shifting things, and he refused to get in the way, despite how difficult the decision proved to be. He asked us to pray for him right then and there. That day I saw his vulnerability and realized that he didn't care about his title or all the accolades. All that Pastor Craig wanted to do was hear from God and be obedient. He has always been transparent in his leadership and willing to share his heart. He has not lost his ability to relate to those around him.

As the time arose for me to start leading others, I remembered these lessons. I was really struggling with enlarging my vision. I didn't know if I could be relevant in this setting. Coming from a midsized suburban church to Lakewood, I had no choice but to challenge my thinking and seek the "God Idea" versus the good idea. I had to step out and change my perspective. There is so much freedom when you begin to tap into the mind of Christ.

A leader is said to be one who goes before others and shows the way. Pastor Craig exemplifies this, modeling the words that he speaks. As both an intern and now a staff member, I have worked with Pastor Craig, never once seeing duplicity in his character. He is the same in the pulpit, with his family and with the staff he oversees. To this day he still stops me in the hall to encourage me, and I still feel as valued as the first day I arrived. Pastor Craig has shown me the value of integrity, honoring and encouraging others, and empowering and releasing others into their full potential. I count it a privilege to serve under a man who has resolved to devote himself to the building of God's kingdom.

QUESTIONS FOR ACTION

1. Do you easily seek help from others or do you normally do things on your own? Why do you think that is?

2. How would developing the heart of a child influence your effectiveness as a leader?

3. Think of someone you know who has the will of a warrior. What words best describe that person?

4. Consider a time when your thoughts or fears paralyzed you from doing something great for God. What would you do differently?

5. As you consider the story of coming to Lakewood, reflect on which vertical leaders have helped you see God's purpose for your future.

6. What steps can you take over the next month to develop the heart of a child and the will of a warrior?

Note

1. John Osteen, "Developing Miracle-Working Faith," sermon delivered in Fall 1996.

3

Destiny Seeds

God is positioning you right now to profoundly impact someone you have yet to meet. When it happens, you will remember this message and know that nothing happens by accident!

Have you ever wondered how a tiny seed can produce so much beauty? Who would guess that something so small and seemingly insignificant could be one of God's greatest inventions? Yet miraculously, a tiny seed carries nutrients powerful enough to create and sustain a vibrant life. Once planted and watered, a seed you might have overlooked breaks out of its shell to become a living organism.

Plants share common characteristics with other living things. Just like human beings need to breathe, a plant needs to breathe. Just as the human body is comprised of cells, plants also have cells that ultimately generate the structure for something brilliant to be released. God doesn't give us seeds without growth potential. When God plants, He plants with the knowledge that greatness already lives and breathes within the seed. Where others don't see the potential, God already sees the end result. Scientists understand that within the nucleus of atoms lies incredible power. When combined with other ingredients, formidable reactions can take place. There is also great power in the nucleus of the seeds God plants. When nurtured, these seeds can cause a reaction that can change the world.

God has planted inside each person what I call "destiny seeds." Destiny seeds contain God's vision for your life: your potential, your talents, your calling. God gives us destiny seeds before we are born. Knowing the gifts and talents He has planned for you, God crafted seeds specifically designed to cause a chain reaction in your life. We are each made in God's own image, so we know that excellence has been embedded in our DNA. Destiny seeds carry the ingredients from which leaders are made, and when activated, new leaders are born. English author Samuel Johnson once said, "Your aspirations are your possibilities." These aspirations are passed from generation to generation through the will of individuals who pursue their God-given destiny.

I've always been impressed by handmade quilts. Each one has a unique design carefully woven together by a master quilter who has learned techniques and style from a rich history of quilting. In a similar way, our lives have unique designs woven by the meticulous hand of God. God creates our design through a rich history of leaders in our lives. Just as a quilt is designed to not only be colorful, but also to keep us warm, you were designed for a purpose. You've been given "threads" in your life that will be passed on to help shape the quilt of your life. Those threads represent your investment in others. When those in whom we have invested live out their purpose, they too will invest in new leaders and help them pass on new threads to others. It's a process that is passed on from generation to generation. It's our job as leaders to sew the threads that shape someone else's destiny.

Dad, Baseball and Destiny

My father was an avid baseball fan. The New York Yankees were his favorite team, and his favorite player was Mickey Mantle. When Mickey told America to eat Wheaties, my dad thought his hero was talking directly to him through the television. My father begged his mother to buy him Wheaties so he could play baseball like Number 7. Dad not only ate his Wheaties like Mickey, but he also drank his Yoo Hoo Chocolate Soda like Mickey and talked with a Southern drawl like Mickey. He even ran like Mickey, with his shoulders back and hands to his side. My father eventually played Little League, Pony League, and high school baseball. He even had the opportunity to pitch against Hall of Famer Tom Seaver, who went on to pitch for the New York Mets. Without realizing it, the New York Yankees and Mickey Mantle nurtured destiny seeds in my father's life: God's vision for a father and son.

My dad was a life-long Yankees fan and took me along for the ride. Growing up in northern California, I wanted to root for the Oakland A's, but my dad's stories about Mickey and the Yankees were too hard to resist; and because I wanted to be like my dad, I began to follow the Yankees.

When my son Cory was born, the first thing I bought him was a Yankees cap. Cory heard stories of Mickey Mantle and other great players, and he, too, became a Yankees fan. A few years before my father's death, all three of us went on a baseball road trip. Three generations of Yankee fans watched games at Yankee Stadium, visited the Baseball Hall of Fame, and drove to Baltimore's Camden Yards to see the place where Babe Ruth grew up. All of this happened because Mickey Mantle told a little boy to eat his Wheaties.

Every time my father told me a story or played baseball with me, he encouraged what I have become today and will be until the day I die: a full-blown, die-hard, pin-stripe-wearing, Yankee-loving, baseball fan for life. I'm not a Yankee fan for life because of the New York Yankees; I'm a Yankee fan because my dad's hero planted a seed inside of a little boy who passed that seed on to another little boy who is currently passing that seed on to the next generation.

Who benefited? Well, of course the New York Yankees have made a lot of money from all the T-shirts, baseball caps, tickets

and posters we've bought throughout the years. Yet, the real bene-
factors are my family. My dad and I never had a tough time communicating in my teen years. If we got stuck, we could always talk
baseball. Each generation in my family, from my father to my son,
has played baseball, and we have great memories of family days at
the ballpark. The road trip that my dad, my son and I took was, for
me, the single greatest experience between fathers and sons.

These things didn't just happen. I believe God wanted my family to connect and create memories that would last a lifetime. My
dad's love for baseball watered God's seed of a father and son relationship. Just as my dad before me, I, too, use baseball to build
a relationship with my son. To lead another life, one must be willing to give up a part of his or her own.

Following God's Planting Pattern

Way back in the beginning, God planted destiny seeds in the life of
Abraham. God chose Abraham to be the father of many nations
and a blessing to the world. Abraham planted those same seeds
into his son Isaac, who planted the promise in Jacob. This process
continued for years; and thousands of years later, I'm carrying that
same seed as I write this chapter: God's vision that the whole world
would be blessed. Bryan Houston from Hillsong Church in Australia says that as in biblical times, the seed of spiritual destiny and
potential is carried from generation to generation.[1]

God has stored within each of us destiny seeds that will bring
forth extraordinary results when planted and nurtured. These
seeds, God's vision for our lives, have breakthrough results when
cared for on a daily basis. When we think of destiny, we usually
think of the end result. With a seed, you can't see the end result
right away, but you can see the growth that will ultimately make
your destiny a reality. Destinies do not just happen. You have to

look every day for new opportunities to help those around you reach the promise God has destined for their life. You may never know the impact of your deposit into their lives, but your descendants will carry that seed with them wherever they go.

Planting Seeds: Giving the Glory to Others

How do vertical leaders nurture the seeds that God has planted in others? When you give up part of your own glory so that others might shine, you are leading vertically. When I plant a seed in someone else and teach him or her to do the same, destiny seeds multiply. It takes courage and humility to set aside your own glory, but vertical leaders find glory in the dreams of others. True power in leadership comes when a leader, refusing to allow pride to rule him, helps others succeed. To speak the language of team, one has to believe that everyone plays a part and no one is more important than another.

Every human being is unique and adds value; it's not about strong wills or who gets the praise. Someone once said, "It is amazing how much you can accomplish when no one cares who gets the credit." This is where the first becomes last because someone actually cares about the last person in line. It's a state of mind that can only come from the state of the heart.

A while back, I caught the end of the biggest race in NASCAR: the Daytona 500. Tony Stewart was ahead of Ryan Newman, and Newman wasn't going to catch him if he didn't get some help. Newman's teammate, Kurt Busch, was coming up fast behind him; but instead of trying to pass, he gave Newman a push from behind that catapulted him into the lead just in time to cross the finish line. When asked after the race about his win, Newman said, "I couldn't have done it without my teammate. Most guys would never have done something so unselfish, and I can't thank him enough." Ryan Newman will never forget that Kurt Busch helped him reach his dream of winning the Daytona 500. Next time Kurt Busch needs help, who do you think will be the first one to step up? Ryan Newman. That's the power of team building!

You might ask, shouldn't a leader be driven to achieve all that God has for him or her? Shouldn't we maximize our potential? Yes and no. We can only reach so high on our own, but when we help others reach their potential, everyone benefits. Imagine if we believed that a leader is great not because of who they are, but because of the team they build.

When I look at leaders, I look first at the army of people who believe in their cause. What have they deposited into others? When leaders raise others up, they don't lose anything. The leaders rise higher, the company grows stronger and people take ownership for the team. The more destiny seeds you plant, the better leader you become. Why? Great leaders leave great legacies.

My Father's Greatest Legacy

My father's love for the Yankees was just a small part of his destiny. While Mickey Mantle influenced my dad's love for baseball, someone less famous planted a much bigger seed in my father's life.

My dad's parents migrated from the dust bowls of Oklahoma during the Great Depression to find work in California. They came to live in a two-room shanty on the banks of the Stanislaus River. Two of their five sons died before their first birthday. Working in the fields and orchards, my grandparents picked whatever crops were in season. Times were hard, and many days ended with the disappointment of knowing there was never enough. After binge drinking on a hot summer day, my grandfather wandered out into the river. Unable to handle the strong current, he drowned, leaving my grandmother alone with three young boys, no money and little hope. Not knowing what else to do, she knelt beside her bed and promised God that if He would help her and her babies, she would serve Him for the rest of her life.

A preacher in town, by the name of Charles Sandifer, read about Grandmother's plight in the local newspaper and decided to plant a destiny seed in the life of that broken family. He went down to that little shanty and let the young mother know that everything was going to be okay. His church paid for my grandfather's funeral and brought them food. Taking a special interest in my grandmother's three-year-old son, the pastor became a mentor to him. Every day he planted another destiny seed in my dad's life. The deposits made by that dear pastor changed my dad's life forever.

My father later became a minister who preached around the world and impacted thousands of lives. My dad's mentor saw each day as an opportunity to sow into my father. My father then sowed into my sister and myself so that we could follow our dreams to help others know God. These are the same dreams birthed in previous generations, all the way back to Abraham and David. Galatians 3:29 says, "If you belong to Christ then you are Abraham's seed, and heirs according to the promise." Now there is a whole generation of pastors and leaders in our family that are able to impact more people than my father or his mentor could have ever imagined. Abraham and David didn't know that the destiny seeds they planted would revolutionize the world so that others might be saved. When we make every day our masterwork, we plant destiny seeds that will carry from one life to the next, from one generation to the next.

Are you the leader of a large corporation? You're able to have a tremendous positive impact on those you lead by nurturing the seeds God has stored in their lives. Are you a parent? Then you've been given a unique opportunity to help shape the lives of your children by discovering their gifts and talents and setting them on a course for success. Do you lead a ministry team? God has placed before you a field of seeds to be nurtured. Take a moment to reflect on whose destiny you've been called to nurture.

Tending Your Own Soil

Once you've determined where to plant destiny seeds, the next step is to determine how to plant them. Once, when I planted flowers, I thought I had done everything right, packing the dirt carefully and laying mulch around each plant. But soon weeds started popping up anyway. I tried to pull the weeds and ended up making a huge mess of my nicely manicured lawn. My friend Clayton told me that my first mistake was how I planted the flowers. If I had laid down plastic over the dirt and then planted the flowers in holes, the weeds wouldn't have been able to break through to choke the flowers. Now I would have to plant and lay mulch all over again. Knowing how to plant is as important as knowing where to plant. When we plant the wrong way, weeds can choke the very best things we have planted.

How do vertical leaders plant most effectively? They begin with their own lives. When they pursue God's best, allowing their own destiny seeds to be nurtured, they are in a better position to plant seeds in others. Before you can build teams and plant in the lives of others, you need to make sure that you've prepared the soil in your own life.

Most children's ministries run with few staff members and are dependent on volunteers. It is a huge challenge to find enough volunteers. Leaders feel undermanned and underresourced, and many times underappreciated. In their desperation, many leaders have the following requirements for volunteers:

1. Breathing
2. Breathing with a steady pulse
3. Breathing with a steady pulse and a safe background check

If volunteers fulfill those three requirements, they are in!

At Lakewood, we faced the possibility of gaining 1,500 additional kids when we moved into our new building. Prior to the move, we had 330 volunteers. In order to accommodate possibly 4,000 kids, we needed to recruit approximately 700 volunteers in 12 months. I don't know about you, but I had never done that before on any team in my entire ministry. Not even close. I didn't know how we were going to do it. I had never seen it done by another children's ministry, but I knew kids were going to be turned away if we didn't respond to this unparalleled challenge. The first thing I felt was fear. We were changing so much and laying out such a huge vision I honestly wasn't sure how it could happen. I needed to tend the soil of my own heart. Before I could encourage others to see God's vision, I needed to see it myself.

Because I believe that fear should never hold me back from the best God has for me, I began quoting 2 Timothy 1:7: "For God has not given us a spirit of fear, but of power and of love and of a sound mind" (*NKJV*). I had to get the mind of God, not the mind of Craig. Too many times we let our mind determine the outcome, when God's mind is already made up. God already knows He can do it; He's just waiting for us to make up our mind that He can do it. We have to flip the switch to illuminate our thinking. So I began to think about how great God is. I turned my focus away from my problem and reflected on how God views human beings. I imagined God creating the stars, each one unique and full of power and potential. I reflected on the fact that God has created each person as a creative, gifted, talented champion. If God views me that way, then I need to convey that message to our team.

When we reflect on God's view of people and we see the worl
from His perspective, we are removing the weeds that choke ou
what's possible. I was getting rid of the weeds. When my heart wa
ready, I was able to plant destiny seeds in others. The light canno
come on in another person's life until someone flips the switch. W
have to ask ourselves how many switches we can flip today.

Planting Seeds

At the first team meeting of Kidslife, I began to speak those vertica
thoughts to our leaders. As I built into my leaders, they began to ge
excited, inspired and ready to take on the world. Little did I kno
that, as I built into them, God was building into me. In fact, I was a
shocked as anyone in the room when I said, "Because of the amaz
ing team God has put together, and with God's help, we are going t
recruit and train 670 new leaders for a total of 1,000 leaders befor
we move to the new building." A hush came over the room. Yo
would have thought someone had just danced naked on the stag
Some laughed, some clapped and some just shook their heads. I sav
a couple of them mouth, BY NEXT YEAR?! I suddenly knew tha
most of them felt there was no way it could happen.

In that moment, I faced a critical decision faced by all vertica
leaders who see things from God's perspective: When you don't hav
the support of those you are leading, do you respond to the crow
or do you continue to pursue the vision? Vertical leaders keep build
ing up even when it looks like everything is falling down aroun
them. If you are looking for someone else's stamp of approval, th
validation you are looking for may not be worth the cost of th
stamp. You are already approved by God!

I would rather be optimistic and considered foolish than pes
simistic and considered smart. As a vertical leader, it's your job t
help your team believe that God can do it. At that moment, I neede

to nurture the greatness that already existed in my team. God had already planted within them the ability to take on what seemed like an impossible task.

Our first step was to develop a plan to make the vision a reality. We started by training the leaders to stop sounding desperate when they were recruiting. No one wants to join desperation; they want to join excellence. So even if we weren't one of the best children's ministries in the country yet, we cast a vision of excellence. We were going to look at Kidslife as a church within a church, intertwined with the heart and vision of Pastor Joel and Lakewood.

The first department we wanted to create in Kidslife was our own human resources department. We would build a team whose sole focus was to bring new people in on a constant basis to work with the team leaders in each area. We set up recruiting stations throughout the church with a campaign centered on being a hero to the kids of Lakewood. We designed incentive programs to inspire our leaders to talk to their friends about Kidslife. Launching a Teenlife program to disciple and train young people in leadership, we managed to recruit more than 200 teens that first year. When we moved into the new building one year later, we had our first meeting with more than 800 volunteers. In one year we built a team of more than 1,000 Kidslife volunteers; and when the doors opened to the new Lakewood Church, our Kidslife attendance grew by 1,500 kids. We did the improbable and God did the impossible!

As a result of this experience, I, and the other volunteers, do not walk in fear. In fact, we see the impossible as just another challenge to be met by knowing God's vision, understanding His plan and working hard to make it happen. All this began after I tended the soil of my own fear and came to see the task with God's vision, not my own.

Knowing Who You Are

In addition to tending your own soil, you also need to understand who God has specifically made you to be. Leadership is about knowing who you are without being defensive about who you are not. Despite your gifts and abilities, you can never be all things to all people.

Rick Warren says that if you don't decide who you are, someone else will.[2] God has a plan for your life, but so does everybody else. Vertical leaders don't tell someone what he or she *should* be; they show someone what he or she *can* be. Each leader has one primary objective: to make "team" the number-one cause. You can't build a great team unless you are willing to trust them. Your team will never fulfill their God-given destiny unless each leader intentionally reaches out to help others find their destiny.

God has predetermined that when you live in Him and He lives in you, greatness is flowing in your bloodline. Coming from a royal lineage, you have nobility within you! What fulfills your soul will ultimately be what sustains your life. What sustains your life will ultimately be what controls your destiny.

Oliver Wendell Holmes once said, "What lies behind us and what lies ahead of us are tiny matters compared to what lives within us." You are a child of the Most High God. You already are destined to a life of victory; all you have to do is believe and initiate your destiny. You might hear people say, "I've made too many mistakes already and I'm not sure I can carry on that legacy." Remember, though, what takes man a hundred years to do, God can do in a split second. God will accelerate the process whenever you are willing to make a change. When building leaders, you are creating a path for those you lead to go out and do what they were born to do. What you build in others can change the course of history, because the leaders you've inspired will make history.

Looking Up from the Trenches

Sunni Miles
Lakewood Volunteer

As I reflect over the last few years and think of all the great leaders God has placed in my life, my heart becomes so full and my eyes weep. I believe these leaders were given to me with the purpose of helping me discover a call I never believed I was good enough to receive.

I met Pastor Craig when I was 20 years old. I came to Houston to help my close friends Clayton and Ashlee move in and paint their new home. Pastor Craig came over with a housewarming/birthday present for Ashlee: a cactus! Talk about irony. During our visit, he planted a destiny seed that would eventually flourish into my living out my dream. He told me, "Now is the time to run after God with everything you have. You're young, not married, no kids . . . the time is now! Run after God and He will not disappoint you!" I've never forgotten those words.

A few years went by, and then I received a phone call from Ashlee about the internship at Lakewood. After much prayer, I knew God was calling me to Houston. When I ran after God, my life turned positively upside down and my mindset flipped about how to do ministry!

As I began my internship, I heard phrases like "You will get out of this what you put into it," "You will reap what you sow," and "When you truly put your heart into something, God is going to give back 100 times over." Under Pastor Craig's leadership I grew so much! I learned how to lead my team as a shepherd and to love them as God does. I've learned the dangers of leadership and the temptations the devil uses to trip you up, and also how to fight those temptations. I grew in the art of intentional leading: What you are you will produce, and we must not only cast a vision but also be able to take them there.

My leadership mindset changed with the knowledge that we are to build people, not the programs. God is in the building *people* business. I love the Kidslife motto, "It's a process," and it has helped me in many frustrating times. Being able to be a part of the beginning stages of Kidslife and watching God grow different things from the ground up was such an incredible experience and has helped me trust the process and that all things really are possible with God. When we give our little, God gives much! He'll take our natural and His super and make it supernatural! Something that Pastor Craig has said to me a few times that relieves the pressure of ministry is, "How do you know that God is in control? Because you're not worried about anything."

I've definitely had challenges. But because God surrounded me with so many vertical leaders, when I fell, I was able get back up and charge ahead. The leadership team held me to a level of excellence, and at the same time allowed me to not have to be perfect. I learned the valuable lesson of vulnerability, the love of my leadership and of God's strength.

Pastor Craig has a way of making you know that you are family! The Kidslife team is a family! Even though I'm no longer with the Kidslife team, I still feel very much a part of this family. We experienced life together! We laughed and cried together, went through triumph and heartache, and we truthfully prayed and encouraged one another. Our team created a place where you didn't have to hide struggles or concerns. We helped each other and had an environment that met spiritual as well as physical needs for one another.

When I graduated from two years of the Lakewood Church Internship, I was given the opportunity to "cut the ropes of my boat from the dock" and soar on my own eagle wings to be a children's pastor in Scottsdale, Arizona (hence the irony of the cactus 5 years ago). And although it was hard to leave my Kidslife family, I knew the destiny seeds that were planted in me were beginning to come to fruition! It was my turn to plant those destiny seeds into the next generation. Time to cheer on my team members and believe God for great things! As I left Lakewood, I remembered what I learned from Pastor Craig: that it's never about me and what I can do or accomplish but what my team—through God and only God—can do together. He always told us that you are only as strong as your team and that the goal is never more important than the people. Pastor Craig could walk around a church of 40,000 people, greeting almost everyone by name. He would always remember our recent conversations and encourage us to pay attention to our team as well. He would ask hard questions and was never afraid to tell you what he felt God was saying. He is personal and genuine. He is authentic and touchable. I thank God for Pastor Craig and for the many destiny seeds he planted in my heart, as a leader and as a friend.

QUESTIONS FOR ACTION

1. How does the idea that each person has destiny seeds within him or her influence the way you view those you are called to lead?

2. Make a list of the people who have had a tremendous impact on you and describe how that happened.

3. Would you describe yourself as someone who easily gives glory to others, or as someone who seeks his/her own glory? Why do you think that is?

4. Determine what type of legacy you hope to bestow on your team, and develop a plan to pursue it.

- Are you pursuing God's best in your own life? What changes can you make this week to help you see reality from God's perspective instead of your own?

- What talents/gifts have been planted in you that inform your identity as a leader?

- Make a list of the members of a team that you presently lead. Identify one talent/gift of each member and identify what you can do over the next month to encourage that talent/gift.

Notes
1. Brian Houston, *How to Flourish in Life* (Australia: Maximised Leadership, 2003), p. 7.
2. Rick Warren, "Foundations of Leadership," sermon given in 2005.

4

The Influence of Inspiration

A signature is a unique ID showing you have been there and made your mark. When you impact people in a positive way, it's like signing your signature across their hearts.

In the movie *Mr. Magorium's Wonder Emporium*, the young apprentice Mahoney works for Mr. Magorium in a magical toy store. Confronted by his imminent death, Mr. Magorium intends to leave the store to Mahoney so that she can continue to inspire the children who enter its magical world. Mahoney, who wants to be a great composer, wants nothing to do with managing the toy store.

Throughout the movie, Mr. Magorium finds creative ways to show Mahoney that she has yet to compose her greatest masterpiece: *life*. Just as a book is worthless if not read, a toy store is worthless if not believed in. With Mahoney's confidence waning, Magorium speaks a profound truth: "Life is an occasion, rise up to it." Mahoney realizes that faith in herself is what she needs to bring the magical store back to life. Mr. Magorium's life and enthusiasm helped her to believe and become who she was meant to be.

Leading with Life

Have you ever met an inspired leader who lived and breathed every word spoken and lived every mandate given? Maybe you've watched a leader take a chance on someone no one else believed in, and great things happened. Or maybe a leader with X-ray vision saw things in you that no one else could. Because their actions and words were consistent, you were inspired to be more than you thought possible.

You are where you are today because someone challenged you to reach higher than where you were standing. They taught you not to stand flatfooted, but on your tiptoes. They taught you to jump as high as you could, and if that wasn't good enough, they would get on their hands and knees so you could stand on their back to reach your dream. They never quit or said it was too hard, and they never lost hope, because they saw things from God's perspective.

In prison for teaching others how to experience God's best, the apostle Paul could have found many reasons to complain and give up on his mission. But Paul understood the secret to living as an inspired leader: vertical thinking. In a letter to his friends in Philippi, he wrote:

> I know what it is to be in need, and I know what it is to have plenty. I have learned the secret of being content in any and every situation, whether well fed or hungry, whether living in plenty or in want. I can do everything through him who gives me strength (Phil. 4:12-13).

As an inspired leader, Paul looked up to find the strength he needed, and then he reached out to inspire others. His life and words were consistent; he called others to look up for help, and he lived his life as one who believed what he said. While in prison, many of the guards came to know God's love because Paul couldn't help but inspire others. When life gave him a prison cell, he turned it into a church! Inspired leaders carry the weight for the masses because they realize that God is carrying them. Personally, one of the first times I remember being inspired happened to be through a leader who influenced millions.

The Dream that Never Dies

In 1976, my history teacher introduced our class to Dr. Martin Luther King Jr. Matching the demographics of the primarily Caucasian neighborhood, our school had no African-American students. Personally, I knew nothing about racism and segregation. Yet, when our class listened to a speech given by Dr. King at the Lincoln Memorial, my eyes were opened to the burden others had carried for years. I looked at my friend whose family came from Central America, and I realized that he experienced the same inequality that Dr. King experienced. I could barely contain my emotions when I heard Dr. King proclaim:

> I say to you today, my friends, even though we face the difficulties of today or tomorrow, I still have a dream. It is a dream deeply rooted in the American dream. I have a dream that one day this nation will rise and live out the true meaning of its creed. We hold these truths to be self-evident: that all men are created equal. I have a dream today.[1]

After listening to the speech with the crescendo of "free at last, free at last, thank God almighty, we are free at last," I looked at freedom in a whole new way. Dr. King inspired me to look at my friend and myself in a different way. It was not just the passionate words that were spoken, but also the life he lived. It was clear to me that no matter what happened, Dr. King would pursue his dream. And I was inspired to pursue that dream with him.

A few months later, a new family moved into the community, with a single mom who had adopted an African-American son, a Chinese son and a Caucasian daughter. To say that their family was unusual in our town was an understatement! I invited the older son to play baseball, and we quickly became best friends. Over the years his family experienced prejudice and criticism, but my friendship with David never waned. Thanks to the seeds planted by Dr. King, our relationship was not based on the color of our skin but rather on the "content of our character." Dr. King inspired me to have X-ray vision and see who David really was.

Do you want your life to be an agent of change, inspiring others to become who God created them to be? God has given you the resources you need to live a life that matches your beliefs. You can do all things through the One who strengthens you.

Inspiration to Transformation

Inspiration when acted upon leads to transformation. As a leader, your motive impacts the kind of transformation that takes place. When motivated by your own glory, success will be temporary at best; but when motivated by love, success is guaranteed. What drives the vertical leader is not the response that one's deeds may bring, but the love that allows the words to encourage. Dr King wrote, "Power at its best is love implementing the demands of justice. Justice at its best is love correcting everything that stands against love."[2] Why would someone go out of his or her way to right the wrong of an adversary or bring healing to the soul of a stranger? We were created to stand on the side of love and to help others become all that God has for them. When we know the love that God has for us, we are empowered to go out and inspire others.

Throughout the Bible, God's love motivates the most unlikely people to become agents of change. An outcast woman drawing water at a well became the first missionary. Jesus' actions and words communicated to her that she was accepted and loved. Amazed, she was inspired to share with others. Many believed in Him because of her witness (see John 4).

Nehemiah, the king's cupbearer, understood he was dispensable. His job included tasting the king's food to protect the king from poison. While the culture did not value him, God used him to inspire his people to rebuild a city that had crumbled. His love for God and desire to see God's glory restored inspired others. Both the city and the people of Israel were transformed because of Nehemiah's motivation to please God by doing what seemed impossible (see Neh. 1-6).

Love and determined faith can change lives.

Faith, Hope and Love Can Change a Life

My sister was born with a rare handicap called skeletal dysplasia. She had no kneecaps, and her legs could not bend downward. She could actually touch her forehead with her toes because her legs bent backward. The doctors gave her a 99 percent chance of never walking. She was studied and tested like a guinea pig in hopes of finding a cure. She had multiple surgeries, each beginning with hope and ending with disappointment as the possibility of walking became more unlikely. At one point, the doctor gave up and told my parents she would never walk. That same evening, my father was scheduled to speak at church.

Devastated, my parents began the long drive back home, and my father gave up. Deeply hurt, he told my mom that he didn't have the faith to get up there and tell others to believe. My father planned to tell the pastor that he was stepping away from the ministry. My mom listened and silently began to pray.

When they arrived at the church and walked down the center aisle, my dad felt a tug on the back of his jacket. He looked down to see a little girl who handed him a note and said, "God told me to give this to you." He took the note and continued walking toward the platform to tell the minister he was done. Just as he was leaning over to talk with the pastor, he felt God telling him to read the note. Reluctantly, he reached into his pocket and read, "And my God shall supply all your need according to His riches in glory" (Phil. 4:19, *NKJV*). Something happened in that moment—the faith of the child, the hope expressed in those words and the reminder of God's great love overwhelmed my father. He went on that night to preach spontaneously on "the faith of a little child." A pint-sized inspired leader taught my father to never stop believing for my sister.

Six months later, my sister pulled herself up to the side of the sofa and stood for the very first time. A few months later, she took her first steps, and today my sister is an accomplished musician and music director. She plays the piano and organ with legs that were never supposed to reach the pedals. She walks through Costco, her favorite store, religiously every week on the two legs the doctors said would never work. God used an unexpected and inspired leader to encourage my parents to never give up!

Expecting God's Best

To inspire means to touch the imagination of what can be. Hall of Fame college football coach Lou Holtz has been known to say, "To get a win you don't have to be the best team in the country; you just have to be the best team in the stadium." You have to believe for the best. Imagination develops out of our expectations: The inspired leader expects God's best. How do we begin to expect God's best? Our expectations develop out of our attitude and our actions. Inspirational leadership is a manifestation of a life of hope deeply seeded in the fabric of one's belief system. When we develop the attitude that God is more than able to do what we ask, we can begin to imagine possibilities. When we take steps toward the possibilities, our actions reinforce our expectations and our character begins to change.

Initially my father saw no hope for my sister's condition, and his actions reinforced his discouragement. When the little girl gave him the note, his attitude began to change and he reinforced the change by speaking on faith. The act of preaching began to form his character: a character of hope. Thomas Fuller wrote, "Govern your life and thoughts as if the whole world were to see the one and read the other." The inspired leader is one who is conscious that others are influenced not just by our behavior, but also by our inner motives. Our imagination and expectations are crucial forces in impacting others. When you believe that hope is around every corner, others will begin to believe as well. We tend to want to give people the quick line, the profound quote or the antidote for what ails them instead of investing in being a model they can follow.

A Model of Hope

Tony Campolo tells a story in his book *Everything You've Ever Heard Is Wrong* about a drunk who was converted at a homeless mission.[3] Joe seemed to be beyond hope, but everything changed after his conversion. Joe became the most caring person at the mission, spending his days doing whatever needed to be done. Whether it was cleaning up vomit or scrubbing toilets, Joe did what was asked with a smile on his face and gratitude for the chance to help. He could be counted on to feed the feeble men who wandered into the mission, and undress and tuck into bed those who were unable to take care of themselves.

One evening, when the director was delivering an evangelistic message to the crowd of sullen men, there was one who came down the aisle and knelt to pray, crying to God to help him change. The drunk kept shouting, "Oh, God, make me like Joe! Oh, God, make me like Joe!"

The mission director leaned over, saying, "Son, it would be better if you prayed, 'Make me like Jesus!'" The man looked up and asked, "Is he like Joe?"

God has given each of us the ability to be an inspired leader. Joe did not have to wear a cross or write a book to be an inspired leader. It flowed out of who he became. Such inspiration can flow from us as well, but we need to take the initiative. People are looking for leaders to show them a new way of life. We may not be able to change someone else's situation, but we can change their expectations.

As we started our first year at Lakewood, I knew we had to set priorities. Realizing that sometimes volunteer ministry feels more like a job than a great experience, I told our leaders that we have no other resource as important as our volunteers. Many work a full-time job and then invest up to 10 hours a week in the ministry. We do not want them to feel like a number; we want them to feel like a collaborator.

They had to feel not like just another warm body, but like an irreplaceable treasure. We began to pour more into our team meetings to inspire our leaders. Rather than serve a few snacks and tell our leaders to work a little harder, we created theme meetings based on the resources we had. We decorated the stage and tables and brought in a live band for worship. We made videos sharing stories of how important each team member was to us. When we could afford it we served desserts or meals. We held an awards ceremony honoring leaders who were nominated for demonstrating servant leadership in powerful ways. We had a message designed to encourage, inspiring them not only for the ministry, but also in their personal lives.

So many times as leaders we focus on the task rather than investment. Most people are not inspired by tasks; they are inspired by transformation. When they know they are making a difference and they can see the results, you will get long-term warriors instead of short-term workers. Whether your team is 10 or 1,000, the principle is the same: Your team is the priority. We have huge attendance at our team meetings because they know they are going to be inspired and they know they are going to be appreciated and valued. I had a volunteer say to me, "Pastor Craig, you didn't have to do all of this. Thank you so much." Stop doing only what you have to do, and start doing what you don't have to do. When you hear people say, "You didn't have to do that," you know you are doing the little extra that makes a huge difference. They appreciate it because you didn't have to do it, but you did, because they matter.

Inspiration Through Difficulty

Kevin Laue, a six-foot-ten basketball prospect from California, was born with a left arm that ended at the elbow. When Laue was born, the umbilical cord was wrapped around his neck twice, with his left arm caught in between. The circulation to his arm was cut off, which stunted its growth, but its position had allowed blood to reach the brain. "I think I got pretty lucky," Laue said. "My arm saved my life." Most people wouldn't think of it that way. They would think about the loss, not the gain.

Laue's parents did not coddle him. They bought him sneakers with laces and pants with buttons. They signed him up for Little League, where he swung the bat like a polo mallet. When other children were cruel, Laue resorted to humor. When his mother asked him to wash his hands before dinner, he said that wasn't an option.

Laue was cut from his seventh-grade basketball team, but sprouted to six-foot-ten and made varsity in high school. He could palm the ball with his right hand and use his short left arm to clamp the ball. His outlook was inspirational to his coaches, parents and friends. He led vertically by not letting what he didn't have hinder him. His coach said, "He is an amazing dude that everyone should meet just once." Laue was recruited to play division I basketball at the University of Manhattan.

This is what's called divine inspiration. Kevin knew that when you can't change the circumstance, you can change your perspective. The outward can be transformed by the outlook. We can let our scars remind us of how much it hurts, or we can let our scars remind us of how much we have overcome.

I was playing football at school during recess and I went out for a long pass. The bell was about to ring, so it was the last play of the game, and the game was tied. There were no extra points in recess football. So I went deep, and the quarterback hurled a long pass into the end zone. Running to catch up to the ball, I reached my arms out and caught the pass with my fingertips. Touchdown! As I caught the pass, I didn't realize how close I was to the fence, and a wire from the fence caught me just above my eye and ripped the skin wide open. Blood was streaming down my face but I didn't care, because I had caught the pass and scored the touchdown. For days after that, when people saw the scar, they would ask, "Didn't that hurt?" My reaction was, "Yeah, it hurt, but even though I was knocked down, I held on to the ball!"

Do you walk around hiding your scars because you are ashamed of being a victim, or do you tell people that you may have gotten knocked down, but you held on to the ball and got right back up? It's the difference between being a victim or a victor. It's important to live out that example in front of our teams, friends and family.

Finding Inspiration

There is a tremendous power in building leaders who know that faith can make the blind see, even when visual sight is impossible. We do not see with our eyes, but with our beliefs, thoughts and our will to live an inspired life.

Leaders constantly find themselves in need of inspiration. They grow the company only to be drained in the process. They forget to listen to the music that lifts them. With no inspiration we forget to focus on what helped us grow the business or ministry to the level it has reached. I wonder how often people produce results but feel uninspired by the leaders they work for. You go to work every day with an important title but feel unimportant to your boss. Maybe your leader focuses on what's driving his or her passion and never asks what your passion is. Or maybe you're a pastor or executive who can't remember the last time someone took the time to inspire you. You spend your time pouring out, and you hunger for someone to pour in.

From the CEO to the intern, every team member needs to feel inspired to move the company higher. Everyone on the team needs to look for opportunities to lift one another to a higher level. You become what you practice. Inspiration will rarely just fall down from the sky.

My inspiration begins with my faith in God. I know that God cares about everyone, not just me, so every day I ask God for ways I can lift someone else to a higher plane. When I place my feelings in God's hands, He meets me and loves me whether I'm hopeful or discouraged, angry or loving. He strengthens me to love others, no matter how I'm feeling.

Many times, those I inspire return the favor. I spend time with people who speak life into my thoughts, not death. Being honest and telling others when I need to be inspired frees others to also be honest.

I not only surround myself with those who inspire me, but I also go to places that spark my imagination. Because I work with children, I bought a season pass to Disneyland. On my day off I would go to one of the parks to see how they constructed a stage or edited a video. It helped me believe that we could produce something of that quality. Just the atmosphere made me feel like I could dream again. At Kidslife at Lakewood, you can see examples of that inspiration in our productions, the aesthetics and feel of the overall program. A reporter from Houston's Channel 11 called Kidslife "God's Disneyland." Walking through the parks inspired my thoughts of what could be.

What environments or settings trigger your imagination and fuel your spirit? Everyone needs his or her own place of inspiration. Whether it's a church, a friend, a conference or a theme park, try to find what inspires you. You can become a creative think tank and find ways to inspire those you lead. You can either build inspired leaders or expired leaders; the choice is yours.

When I came to Lakewood as the children's pastor, I thought I was coming to inspire families. I had no idea my family were the ones who were going to be inspired. Shortly after we arrived, we noticed changes in our 18-month-old baby, Connor. In the beginning he was responsive, made eye contact, clapped his hands and even said "mommy" and "daddy." But just after his second birthday we noticed him staring off into space for minutes at a time. He stopped making eye contact and became less responsive to us. When he spoke, it was only parroting what we said, and he never played with other children. Connor couldn't tell us what he wanted or how he felt. I wanted to tell him I loved him, but when I gave him a hug or looked in his face, he looked away. There is nothing harder than not being able to connect with your child emotionally. We were devastated, having heard that autism had no cure and there was a 99 percent chance that Connor would be this way for the rest of his life.

I had come to a new church and was overseeing a large staff and volunteer team. I was trying to inspire them, and on the inside I was holding in such hurt. I didn't know if I could be the leader I needed to be for the ministry when I felt so helpless. Yet every week

I heard Pastor Joel tell me that I am more than a conqueror; I'm the head not the tail; I'm well able to succeed; I'm strong in the Lord; I'm a victor and not a victim. It was those constant words of hope that filled the void of my daily thoughts. Slowly my hopelessness began to fade and my God began to show up. He had been there the whole time, but now I allowed Him to enter my circumstances. My perspective changed, and I spoke words of inspiration every time I got down, every time my wife cried and every time I felt like I couldn't breathe because life was so heavy.

Although we had a good idea of Connor's symptoms, we had never had a professional diagnosis. Connor was tested at the Children's Hospital, and I was driving home when I got the call from my wife. Connor was on the autism spectrum between moderate and extreme. I could feel the enemy speak words of despair: Your son is going to be different; you'll never connect with your son; he will always be deficient. I hit the gas in my car, rushed home, ran upstairs to his bedroom and picked him up, saying, "Connor, you are more than a conqueror, you can do all things, you are the head and not the tail, you are well able to succeed, you are strong in the Lord, you're a victor not a victim." The inspiration God poured into Pastor Joel poured into me and rained down over Connor. I refused to accept the results, because my hope had risen higher than my circumstance. The diagnosis was not the final chapter; that chapter has yet to be written.

It's funny how God turns difficult situations around for our good. Connor has become an inspiration to so many people, and he was the inspiration behind the new state-of-the-art facility we opened to help special-needs kids. As I stood in front of the Lakewood Congregation to introduce the new facility, I said, "If being a champion means you have to be the biggest, strongest or the fastest, then my son and the other kids with special needs would not fit that criteria. Yet, God looks at the heart; and when He looks at our kids, He sees champions. Sometimes children with special needs are the last ones remembered in the church. Many of you parents have not been able to go to church for months. You feel forgotten. We have built a facility, trained leaders and designed a program just for our little champions at Lakewood. I know some of you have felt forgotten, but I want you to know today, you're not forgotten anymore." One of our choir directors was sitting in the congregation that night, having brought her son (who recently had had some challenges) to the service, and said she had prayed for God to give them some hope. She said, "Right after I prayed, you walked up and spoke, and we found hope." Inspiration can change the face of desperation in a split second when we look for ways to bring hope into the lives of people.

John 1:4 says, "In Him was life, and the life was the light of men" (*NKJV*). It's not always easy, but nothing good ever comes easy. There were times in our ordeal with Connor that I didn't want to hear "it's going to be okay," because we lived reality every day. Yet, the vertical leader is not just fueled by acceptance of their encouragement. Rejection spurs the vertical leader to creatively find ways to motivate them even more. Thank God for the pesky, persistent vertical leader. They are like cheerleaders at the pep rally, cheering even though the team hasn't won a single game. They believe a win is right around the corner.

Are you the ray of inspiration that people are drawn to, or do you hide your light? You never know what's around the next corner, what's behind the next door or how God will change the situation. When someone shoots an arrow of despair, you are going to raise a glimmer of hope. Inspiration is a language of life, not a mere word to be spoken. It starts with you as a leader. When you shift your paradigm, someone else's life will rise higher, their problems will seem easier and the load will be lighter because you dared to be a vertical leader.

Looking Up from the Trenches

Veronica Montgomery
Lakewood Team Member

On my first day of ministry, Pastor Craig took me to lunch and began asking about my personal life. I was surprised that he was not asking more about my credentials and how I was going to take the ministry to the next level. Instead he asked me about my family, my interests and hobbies! He was asking questions that I felt were insignificant to the ministry. I was so surprised that my boss would care about these details, but by the end of our lunch, I learned an important lesson: He showed me that I was important! In order to take my team to a new level, I was going to have to take the time to build relationships with them in the same way.

I realized that during my first months in the ministry I was going to have to focus on building relationships. I needed to get to know my team on an *intimate level*. I had to know their names, their birthdates, their families, their interests and hobbies. The impact that I leave on the families in the ministry as well as my team is far greater than the programs that I build.

So I began emailing, calling, setting up dinners and meetings with my team just to fellowship with them and know them on an intimate level. I asked personal questions that some may feel are insignificant, but this helped me build strong, lasting relationships that will last. I made deposits in their lives and I knew that I was making a difference. As I started to invest in them, it became easier for me to challenge them. For example, I would ask them to step out of their comfort zone and try different things, and they would take on these challenges because they trusted me. I know they would not have accepted the challenge if I did not take the time to form my relationship with them. Investing time in my team took away their perception of me as a "boss." Instead they saw me as a leader. My team began to *follow me* and not just *do a job* for me because of my title. My team is inspired by me rather than working for me.

Although I was investing in my team and building relationships, I was still insecure about my leadership role. I would question my performance. During these times, Pastor Craig told us about the importance of leading with the mind of Christ. He inspired me with Scripture and examples of how trusting God is so much more important than what we may think is right.

Pastor Craig challenged us to spend time in God's presence daily and to put God first in everything. This gave me so much confidence, because I knew that as I continued to seek Him, He would give me the wisdom I need to make decisions that are pleasing to Him.

QUESTIONS FOR ACTION

1. List three leaders who demonstrate consistency in their words, actions and attitudes. What about their lives inspires you?

2. Does your confidence in God inspire others to believe in God's possibilities? What's one change you could make today to gain a vertical perspective?

3. Describe a situation where love and determined faith inspired others to extraordinary change.

4. Identify a difficult situation in your team. Can you imagine "hope around every corner" as you face this situation? Determine how you will communicate that hope with those you lead.

5. Brainstorm some ways you can inspire your team to feel like a valued treasure. Begin to implement a couple ideas and take notes on the changes you and the team experience.

6. What do you currently do to stay inspired as a leader? Make a list of places and people that inspire you, and develop a plan to regularly gain inspiration.

7. What arrows of despair have you or your team faced recently? Reflect on words of inspiration that have been poured into you that you can also pour into your team.

Notes

1. Dr. Martin Luther King, Jr., "I Have a Dream," speech delivered August 28, 1963, Washington, D.C. http://www.usconstitution.net/dream.
2. Dr. Martin Luther King Jr., *Where Do We Go from Here: Chaos or Community?* (Boston, MA: Beacon Press, 1968). http://www.mlkonline.net/quotes.html.
3. Tony Campolo, *Everything You've Ever Heard Is Wrong* (Dallas, TX: Word, 1992), p. 73.

5

Dream Makers

One of the best parts about those who dream big is that growing old never phases the one whose heart stays eternally young, because each dream carries them into a new adventure where age is irrelevant. Let God give you dreams that will carry you through a lifetime and beyond.

Over the years I have been encouraged and praised many times, but hearing the words "I believe in you" authentically coming from another is a rare treasure. I still remember the first time I heard those words. We were playing our final game of the season for the championship: the Oaks vs. the Beavers. My team, the Oaks, was ahead by one run in the fifth inning of a six-inning game. I had been playing third base for the first five innings when the coach asked me to play left field. My head dropped in shame. I thought he was moving me to the outfield because he was afraid I would cost us the game.

Frustration set in as I tried to figure out why I was being demoted after playing a great game. Coach noticed the look on my face, knelt down and said, "Son, this is the biggest game of the year. The third batter in the line-up has hit a home run already, and I need my best fielder out there. Do you understand why I want you to play left field?" My head shot up and I proudly said, "Yes, sir." As I turned to take off for the outfield, the coach turned me around and said, "Craig, I believe in you."

I ran as hard as I could run to take my spot proudly in left field.

The first batter hit a base hit to center field. The second batter popped it up along the first base side. Next up was the big home-run hitter! I crouched down and waited to see if fate would come my way. After what the coach had said, I could just see myself catching the ball and saving the game. I was dreaming big, and I knew I could do it because my coach believed in me! The first pitch was delivered, and the batter hit a long fly ball down the left field line. I took off as fast as my little legs could go. I reached out with my glove but the ball just missed me. The umpire called out, "Foul ball." Getting back into position I moved toward the left line. The next pitch was thrown: Ball one outside! Ball two, high and outside! I could tell the batter was getting frustrated, because he wanted to win the game for his team. The next pitch comes: ball three! I started to think maybe the coach put me in the outfield for no reason.

By this time the home-run hitter knew he only had one shot, so he lunged at the next pitch, which was high and outside, and sent it straight into the dugout. Our pitcher threw another ball and the home-run hitter walked to first base. *Wait a second,* I thought, *that's not how this is supposed to go.*

The next batter had not managed to get the ball past the infield the entire game. I saw his coach stop and kneel down to talk to him. *No way . . . is he telling him he believes in him too? Is there a believe fest going on? It doesn't matter,* I thought, *he could get the best pep talk in the world but he still wouldn't be able to hit the ball out of the infield.* In the two games we'd played against the team, this player had struggled every time. Yet, after the coach's pep talk, the boy's demeanor had changed; he seemed confident. *Oh great, the coach must have used the magic words, "I believe in you."*

I had eased up in the outfield, fairly confident the ball would never reach me. With similar confidence, the pitcher threw a straight fastball. With a mighty swing the batter missed the ball.

Rearing back, the pitcher hurled in strike two. As he was winding up for his next pitch, I thought, *This will be strike three* . . . when all of a sudden the batter hit the ball to left center field. Surprised, I bolted toward the ball. Keeping my eye on the ball, I made a leap into the fence with my glove arm going over the fence. Just as I was pulling my arm back over, I heard someone shout "Home run!" and the crowd roared. But when I brought my arm over and looked down in my glove, there was the ball! I held it up for everyone to see, and throwing the ball back to first, we got a double play to win the championship game. The crowd went crazy, and even the visiting team stood up and applauded my dream catch. And Coach stood waiting for me by the dugout. He picked me up and swung me around, saying, "I told you that you could do it! Yes!"

It was one of the greatest days of my life because an ordinary coach said four words to an ordinary player and turned him into an extraordinary player. He was a dream maker that day. Through the power of his belief in me, he made one of my dreams come true. Yet, he wasn't the only coach who changed a player's life that day. In the visitor's dugout, the Beavers' coach had his arm around the boy who almost won the game. The boy was crying, but the coach was speaking words of life into the deflated young boy. I believe the coach was telling him that "today was not your day, but your day is coming. Keep your head up. You did something I've never seen you do, and if not for that miraculous catch, you would have won the game." Why do I believe he said something like that? The very next year that boy hit three home runs to win the championship game for his team. His time had finally come.

I Believe in You

Everyone needs someone to believe in him or her. In the book of Exodus, Moses was tending his father-in-law's flock when God decided to put Moses in the game. Moses had never been eloquent; he had a speech impediment and didn't believe he could bring his people out of Egypt. But God said, "I will help you speak, and teach you what to say. Take this staff in your hands so you can perform miraculous signs with it." God wasn't concerned about Moses' disabilities, because He knew Moses' potential. When Moses finally got in the game, he began to perform miracles. Exodus 14:29-31 says that Moses led his people to victory over Pharaoh, and verse 31 tells us that when the Israelites saw the great power of the Lord, they feared the Lord and put their trust in Him and in Moses. God was the dream maker for Moses and his people. God said, "I believe in you, Moses, even if you don't believe in yourself."

If you want to become a great team builder, you have to be more than a leader; you need to become a dream maker. Why? Because building your team from 25 volunteers to 300 doesn't seem realistic when you focus on how difficult the task is. The average leader may settle for just being in the game, never believing that the dream could become reality. We need to change our mindset from administrator to dream maker, from director to dream maker, from employee to dream maker.

I am not just a pastor; God has positioned me to be a dream maker. When I work with a team member, I'm not just interested in seeing that person do the job; I'm interested in seeing his or her dreams come true. If I can be a catalyst for seeing people's dreams become reality, how much more are they going to invest in the goals that our church or company is trying to achieve?

God is positioning you right now to impact someone in a profound way. You could be the dream maker that God uses to make the ordinary into the momentous. So many people have accepted their role in life and have stopped dreaming. They need someone to rekindle the fire and spark the dreams that have gone dark inside of them.

Teaching Someone to Dream Again

A waitress in Texas, Ivory Harlow, became a dream maker for another through a simple act of kindness. Ivory served coffee at a diner and often saw a look of isolation in her customers' eyes. They'd come in the door, sit at the counter and look around for a connection. In the age of online chat, online shopping and even online school, it's no wonder people coming into a diner are starving for human connection. As Ivory serves up their eggs and bacon, the customers offer updates on their grandchildren and ask her about her life.

One day, as she was refilling coffee cups, she saw a woman who had been sitting in a corner booth for at least three hours. The woman looked up and asked, "How much for just one breakfast taco?" Ivory said she'd find out, but as she was walking back to the kitchen, she thought about the woman's rotten teeth and tired eyes, and went back and gave the woman a free pancake breakfast. She fibbed that it was left over from an order she had messed up. The woman asked if she could borrow bus fare, and Ivory handed over her tip money from her apron pocket.

Three weeks later, the woman came back and paid back her $2 loan to Ivory. She had gotten a job and wanted to buy the waitress breakfast on her break! Ivory realized that something as simple as a short stack of pancakes could bring about a small shift in society. Ivory inspired the woman to keep going and pursue the simple dream of having a job. She wasn't just going through her day unaware of her surroundings. She had helped a woman get back on her feet.

People look on the outside, but God looks at the heart. Dream makers see things from God's perspective. They look past the outside and believe when no one else notices. If you want to build great leaders, find out what their dreams are or help them find their dream. When we look for ways to impact our team profoundly, we open the door for them to become impact players. Great team building isn't about the method; it's about meeting the need.

Recently, I was talking to the volunteer coordinator for Texas Children's Hospital. They have more than 800 volunteers serving every month. Teenagers play with sick children in their rooms and adult volunteers run a radio station that helps kids feel special in the comfort of their rooms. A few years ago, I volunteered and spent time reading books with a little boy. I listened to him as he told me all about his favorite superhero, Spiderman. I didn't know the impact I was making until the day when he handed me a drawing of Spiderman. Instead of writing Spiderman at the top of the page, he had written my name. I will never forget how it felt to find out that superheroes don't have to be from far-off galaxies; they can be ordinary people like you and me. When I asked the volunteer coordinator if it was tough for them to recruit such a high volume of volunteers, she told me it was no problem at all. "What is your secret?" I asked her. "There is no secret," she said. "Most of the volunteers are family or friends of kids who have been impacted by the staff and volunteers here. They, in turn, want to impact others."

The volunteers become dream makers for kids and families. You will not be able to contain your volunteers either when they see the impact they can make when they focus more on the people than the program.

Changing Someone's Countenance

One of the ways we build teams is by making our quarterly team meetings an incredible night of thanks and inspiration. One night we put together a meeting we called "Dream." The room was decorated to give the impression that you were sitting in a white cloud surrounded by stars. Three months earlier the team had met to plan our entire year's schedule. Our calendar meetings are like spiritual brainstorming sessions: we never know where things will lead. That year prophetic words emerged such as "Move out of the way," "Unity," "Trust God" and "I have empowered and equipped you to do great things." Two Scriptures emerged to set the tone for our meeting. One was Jeremiah 29:11: " 'For I know the plans I have for you,' declares the Lord, 'plans to prosper you and not to harm you, plans to give you hope and a future.' " The second Scripture was Habakkuk 2:2-3. In this passage, God answers Habakkuk's dream that justice would be done to end the struggle of corruption in Judah: "And then God answered: 'Write this. Write what you see. Write it out in big block letters so that it can be read on the run. The vision-message is a witness pointing to what's coming' " (*THE MESSAGE*).

We knew that many of our leaders had not dreamed in a long time. We knew that some of our leaders were tired, some were struggling with family issues, and some had always taken care of others and had forgotten how to dream for themselves. We put the prophetic words and the Scriptures on a credit-card-sized key ring card along with the word "Dream." It was a reminder for them to never stop believing or dreaming.

We started the night by sharing the dreams for Kidslife and what we wanted to do in the year to come. Everyone cheered and showed excitement about the vision. Then I said, "The dreams of Kidslife are important, but I don't want just the dreams of Kidslife and Lakewood to come true. We want to know what your dreams are and how we can partner with you to help your dreams come true. Some of you have never had anyone ask you what your dreams are. Some of you have put your dreams on the shelf to take care of others. Tonight, we want to begin seeing your dreams become reality. Your dreams are not in your past but in your future. We want to help some of you dream bigger, and we need to help some of you begin to dream again."

As I was speaking, I could see the parents of a child with autism begin to weep. I saw others smiling. They'd thought I was just going to tell them the goals we had for Kidslife. A sense of love filled the room as they began to write out their dreams on the Dream Cards and place them at the center of the table. As a team, we spoke words of encouragement and prayed that God would see these dreams and bring them to pass in the future. One of our volunteers who has a son with Down syndrome said, "I don't think I ever thought about what my dreams were until tonight. This is the first time someone has asked me. Thank you."

Over the next few months we began getting emails of dreams coming true. One of our staff members had dreamed of having a little baby girl. When she became pregnant later that year, the report came back that she was having a baby girl. Another woman had been praying for years that her brother would turn away from gangs and drugs and give his life to God; that year it came to pass. We know there will be more reports to come. That night, our team moved to a whole new level. In one night we saw people's countenances change. We launched a new program and added 150 new volunteers. A sense of servanthood and unity sprang forth and the whole feel of our ministry was changed.

Putting Others' Dreams Before Your Dreams

A year before that team meeting, God began to speak to me about how I was coveting my ministry. I was so focused on the vision and my team that at times I forgot the teams around me. When I first came to Lakewood, one of our strengths was that we acted like one big team. Kidslife was able to grow so quickly because we partnered with the other ministries of the church. I sensed God saying that if I humbled myself and offered my help to the other ministries of the church, He would take Kidslife to a whole other plane. It was freeing.

Ministries within a church can get competitive. Ministries unintentionally jockey for space, resources and leadership. Despite having just moved into a huge facility, Lakewood was already struggling to find enough space for all of the ministries' needs. When I began to share my focus with other ministries that needed help, Kidslife began to see great things happen. We lifted up the youth department, and a stronger unity began to flourish. Whenever we were asked to speak or partner with the other leaders, it became a privilege, not a burden. We planned mission trips together and we worked hard to share space. We sought to make every situation work out to be a win-win.

You might think that by taking some focus off Kidslife and putting it on other ministries, our production and impact would go down. Just the opposite happened. We not only continued what we were doing, but we also started multiple new ministries within Kidslife. It's not that you let go of your dreams; it's that you don't let your dreams become your idol. James 4:6 says, "God opposes the proud but gives grace to the humble." Matthew 23:12 says, "Whoever exalts himself will be humbled, and whoever humbles himself will be exalted." Dream makers think not only of their own dreams, but they also put the dreams of others first. They know that God makes our dreams a reality when we put others first. Don't be driven by success; everyone has a different idea of what success looks like. Always be driven by being fulfilled. Success brings short-lived happiness; fulfillment brings long-term joy.

Vertical leaders create a place for extraordinary change in their organization because they take time to understand the dreams of those they lead. When people know that you have their best interests at heart, and that you believe in them, they will not only appreciate you as a leader but they will also follow your lead. A culture of trust and support will develop that will literally take your organization to the next level. Would you like to see God's best in your life?

Become a Dream Maker!

Looking Up from the Trenches
Clayton Hurst
Lakewood Team Member

During the last five years, I feel as though I've been enrolled in an exclusive leadership school. From the very beginning, Craig has gone above and beyond to develop me and many others as great leaders. We have a Kidslife motto that the staff says: "It's a process!" One thing we've all realized is that it is going to take some time to get where we want to be. It's going to be a process, so we may as well enjoy it!

Throughout the evolving process of Kidslife, one of Craig's leadership lessons that has stuck out to me is being a student of human behavior. Within Kidslife we realized early on that the person was much more important than the program. If we could build up and develop the person, the program would follow. This has helped me enormously in building and developing my teams. When you can find out from a person what their true strengths and dreams are and then help to develop them, it is so rewarding. I love to see the expression and reaction of people when I ask them what they are passionate about.

One individual stands out to me when I think of the "passion" question. When Becky first came into my office, she was extremely shy and kept her head down. While chatting, I found out that she was a mother of two, and she wanted to learn how to lead and impact kids. As we continued to talk, though, I noticed that she would never look me in the eyes. She would look around the room but would never look at me. Yet her smile would literally light up the room. Her smile and laugh were so contagious that it makes me smile thinking about it two years later. After our initial meeting, we began to put Becky into roles that would challenge her and fulfill her. Because of Becky's passion for impacting kids and families, she began serving in our midweek discipleship ministry for kids. We call it Extreme Kids because we help kids and parents to go extreme for God.

We placed Becky in a group of fourth-grade girls, and after a few weeks had gone by, I noticed something that just about made my mouth drop to the floor. Becky was in a corner with her small group of girls. They were hanging on every word she said, and Becky herself was looking them right in the eye as she shared the lesson. It was an amazing sight and so different from our first conversation in my office that day.

Over the next few weeks, I noticed Becky getting more and more comfortable with her small group. I was so intrigued by this turnaround that I asked Becky to stop by and talk with me. When she came in and sat down, however, something strange happened. As soon as we began to talk, her old tendencies started up again. I would ask a question and she would begin talking and immediately put her head down and never make eye contact. After speaking with Becky, something hit me about her passion and her dreams: She loved helping people. For whatever reason, when she was with that small group of girls the only thing going through her mind was that she was helping each of them. That dream would spur her on, and it was like she became someone else. She was animated and full of life because she was fulfilling her passion.

When we started Kidslife, we purchased some custom mascots to be ambassadors of our children's ministry and help the kids get excited about coming to check us out. The mascots are amazing; each one has its own story about how they came to Kidslife. Due to the size of the mascots, however, we need smaller people or young teens to fit into the suits. We needed more people to get plugged in to our mascots teams, and I got the crazy idea to ask Becky if she would help in the building of these teams. Without hesitation she said yes and was off. She grabbed a stack of applications and informational material and headed over to talk with some teens. Later that night, I saw Becky and asked her how it went. Her response made me so glad that I had asked her what her passion was and didn't look just at how she acted in my office. She said, "Well, I talked to a lot of teens tonight, and 28 of them filled out an application. I was hoping to get a few more, but it's a good start!" Honestly, I was blown away. I asked her, "Becky, how in the world did you get 28 teens to sign up for mascots?" She said, "I just smiled real big, looked them in the eye and asked them!"

Becky is my inspiration to find out about the passions others have and help them reach their dreams!

QUESTIONS FOR ACTION

1. Who believes in you? How has his/her belief in you had an impact in your life?

2. What practical benefits would your organization experience if your team knew you cared about their dreams?

3. What dreams do you have for your organization? Write down your dreams and begin to talk about them with God and with others in your organization.

4. Create a plan to discover the dreams of those you lead and a way to help those dreams become a reality.

5. What can you do over the next year to help other departments in your organization discover and fulfill their dreams?

6

Dream Breakers

If people try to tell you to stop loving, stop believing, stop hoping for the best, or stop caring too much, remember that God isn't holding a stop sign. His name has "Go" in it!

Every December, like most children in America, I looked forward to Christmas. I loved everything about the season: setting up the tree, decorating the house, dropping hints about gifts I wanted and, of course, watching the Christmas specials on television. Back then no one owned them on DVD, so we had to check the *TV Guide* to make sure not to miss the classics like *Miracle on Thirty-Fourth Street*, *Rudolph the Red-Nosed Reindeer* and *It's a Wonderful Life*. One of my all-time favorites was *A Charlie Brown Christmas Special*. Little did I know that Charles Schultz's dream for *A Charlie Brown Christmas Special* was almost squelched because of some well-positioned dream breakers.

When the special was in the last stages of production, the network executives began to express concern. Typical of dream breakers, they saw the problems instead of the possibilities. They complained about choppy animation, poor sound quality and the lack of what was then an industry standard—a laugh track. Charles Schultz believed the audience should laugh when they wanted to and did not need to be prompted. The producer's main concern, which they felt guaranteed the program's failure, was Linus's now-famous rendition of the Christmas story.

The dream breakers were convinced they would lose ratings and corporate sponsors because Americans would not want to spend their prime time listening to a cartoon character quoting the *King James Version* of the Bible. In response to these dream breakers, Charles Schultz, in typical dream-maker fashion, responded, "If we don't tell them the real meaning of Christmas, who will?"

A Dream Breaker

Have you ever had a dream stomped down by someone? Dream breakers use words, like NEVER, IMPOSSIBLE, CAN'T, WON'T, DON'T, STOP or NOT. If anyone has said you'll *never* do that, it's *impossible*, you *won't* reach your goal, you're *not good enough*, those are dream breakers.

The CBS executives were looking to make money, not change lives. Fortunately for every child who has watched *A Charlie Brown Christmas Special*, Charles Schultz saw something greater than just a cartoon. He saw the possibility of impacting a nation. The scene of Linus telling the true story of Christmas was voted by *TV Guide* as one of the top 100 scenes in television history. On the night it aired, most of the nation watched that special. *A Charlie Brown Christmas Special* has won more awards and accolades than any other.

All of us will face dream breakers. Dream breakers are not always bad people. I'll bet most of the CBS executives who were opposed to Charles Schultz at the time can now look back and see their mistake. All of us, at one time or another, have been a little off track and said words that could shatter dreams. What causes good people to break dreams? Pride, ego, jealousy, negativity and a need for control can all cause good people to become dream breakers.

Making History

Vertical leaders build into others by identifying and then getting rid of those things that cause them to become dream breakers.

They look beyond personal feelings in order to see what God might be doing in any particular situation. One way I keep the perspective of a dream maker is by remembering that every day is historic. I've been called by God to make history by building into people's lives, hoping that one day I will hear God say, "Well done, good and faithful servant." When I remember that my life is being recorded in the most important history book ever, the Book of Life, I work to live a life that helps others achieve their God-given purpose.

How do we keep God's perspective and prevent pride, envy, jealousy and negativity from destroying others' dreams? We need to talk with God every day and ask Him to help us keep His perspective. We also need to ask His forgiveness for the times when we've intentionally and unintentionally hurt others. One of the shortest but most amazing verses in Scripture says: "Draw near to God and He will draw near to you" (Jas. 4:8, *NKJV*). You do not have to figure this out on your own. God will create historic days for you as you seek Him every day as a vertical leader.

A Day that Changed My Life

Some people think my greatest times in ministry at Lakewood are when I have the opportunity to speak in the sanctuary to thousands of people. Others might think it's the opportunity to minister to thousands of kids and families every week. Those are tremendous opportunities, but my greatest ministry at Lakewood did not take place within the church walls.

I received a phone call from Dr. Paul Osteen, telling me about a little boy who had tragically lost both his parents. Dr. Paul called to make sure the family and the little boy would experience huge amounts of support and love. Apparently, the father had been angry and distraught, and his depression turned into anger and then to verbal abuse. In the heat of an argument, the father shot the little boy's mother right in front him. Before he turned the gun on himself, he looked at his son and said, "I hate you." If the words "I believe in you" are dream-building words, then the words "I hate you" are dream crushers, especially when they come from the person who is supposed to protect you.

When I showed up at the funeral service, I was told that the mom had occasionally brought the little boy to Kidslife at Lakewood, but I had never met him. My first impression of him occurred at the funeral with his family and friends surrounding him to shelter him from any more damage. Both sides of the family were in attendance, trying to make sense of what had taken place. You could feel the tension and unspeakable hurt. I wasn't sure I would get a chance to speak to him; and even if I did, I could not imagine what I might say in such a terrible moment. During the entire service, my eyes were fixed on that little boy while I focused my mind on God, hoping for words to say. I realized this was a vertical leadership moment unlike any other. As I drew near to God, I could sense that He was drawing near to me.

The service ended and I came down to the front to meet the family and the little boy and offer encouragement, hoping to reverse in some small way the words that had been spoken by his father. I expected the boy to be in shock and bitter about what had happened. Instead, as I reached out my hand to him, the little boy grabbed my hand and then wrapped his other arm around this stranger he had never met. He clung to me like a son hugs a father, with no inhibition. Stunned, I held him like I would hold my own two boys whom I love with my whole being.

Suddenly, I realized what was happening. God had drawn near and was using me to hold His child through my body. Do you want to know why I know this? The first words out of my mouth were, "I love you, son." I did not plan to say that at all. I felt as though God was speaking through me. The next words that came out of my mouth were, "It's okay; I'm here."

Afterward, I felt as though God the Father had been holding His child, telling him that everything was going to be okay. God's plan was to replace every destructive word with victorious words that would heal his heart. The Dream Maker was taking back what the dream breaker had stolen.

I've found in life that you do not have to be present in the battle for God to be there fighting on your behalf. He will take your place. Your faith puts Him in the fight. The battle belongs to the Lord.

A Scripture that I hold on to at times like this comes from one of Jesus' close friends, Peter. It reads:

And the God of grace, who called you to his eternal glory in Christ, after you have suffered a little while, will himself restore you and make you strong, firm, and steadfast (1 Pet. 5:10).

God has promised to restore those whose dreams have been broken. God can and will restore your dreams. As a leader, God calls you to also restore the dreams of those on your team by speaking words of life to them. As you pray and draw near to God, He will begin to help you rebuild areas in your life that have been torn down. As you draw near to Him, watch how He not only heals broken dreams but also uses you to restore others' dreams.

While we might not all have dramatic moments to speak healing words into someone's life, normal moments can often have the greatest impact. The words you use on a daily basis and your actions toward others determine whether you are a dream maker or a dream breaker. As a leader, I have found that the manner in which I try to help someone makes all the difference in the world. Author Napoleon Hill once said, "Think twice before you speak, because your words and influence will plant the seed of either success or failure in the mind of another."

A Word About Constructive Criticism

As a leader, you'll have plenty of opportunities to let others know how they can pursue their dreams in a positive manner. You will need to guard against the trap of constructive criticism. To me, constructive criticism is an oxymoron. We call it constructive criticism when we haven't built a relationship with someone we wish to evaluate. Many times we veil our words with excuses: "I did that for his own good." "I was just speaking the truth." "I'm only telling you this because I care." Critics offer their version of the truth for selfish reasons, not to build people up. The truth hurts when the motive is selfish. But when the truth comes from a heart of love, and when leaders speak truth for the gain of others, people will be set free.

Often the difference between a dream maker and a dream breaker is the relationship. Before we can offer critique or insight into someone else's dream, we need to invest time and energy in them. We need to let others know that we love them and have their best interests at heart. If you don't have relationship with the one you are trying to bring correction to, it will backfire quickly. Correction is more likely to be received well when a relationship is established.

Love takes time. Too often we say "helpful" things before the relationship has developed, and team members are hurt because they do not know our heart. The best way to combat this is to speak words of life and not death. Words of life come from a heart that wants to see others succeed, not to promote our own ideas.

Dream breakers speak words that cause doubt and fear, while the dream maker speaks words of hope and encouragement.

Listening to the Right Voices

Charles Schultz never lost his focus in the midst of some very powerful negative voices. His determination to tell the story of Christmas in a simple yet profound way literally made history. Your focus will determine who you listen to. I see people who live a life so far below their potential because they are listening to voices that have broken their dreams. They stay in jobs and under leaders who impress to oppress. These leaders are never happy, it's never good enough, and they are never for anybody but themselves.

At some point we have to realize that there are always going to be people who are not for us, no matter how hard we try. We have to shake it off and refocus. Don't chase after people who pull you down; chase after people who build you up. Choose to be around people who want to know your dreams so you can dream together. If we settle or accept our lot in life, we will never reach higher than the status quo.

In the song "Meant to Live," by the band Switchfoot, the lead singer screams the chorus, "We were meant to live for so much more . . . have we lost ourselves?"[1] Have you ever found yourself just going through the motions and not living in all that God has for you? After years of trying to please others, sometimes we give up and stop living in our true identity and purpose. We lose the identity and purpose that God gives us when we try to gain the acceptance of others. It's always a mistake to try to make the dream breakers happy instead of seeking to please the One who gave us the dream. Dream breakers can take the form of bosses, parents, negative friends and even pastors.

When we dig down deep and ask God what we are meant to do, we discover our true identity. Our focus shifts from pleasing those who refuse to be pleased, to pleasing the One who already loves us and wants the best for us. When we find our identity as a person and leader in God, we are not as concerned about pleasing dream breakers. Dream breakers are not interested in your life; they are interested in their agenda. You do not have to settle, as a leader, for anything but God's best. You do not have to accept what people say about you when God is for you. You can listen to a million voices or tune into an audience of One.

In the Bible the children of Israel longed to enter the Promised Land. After being set free from slavery they were ready for a place to settle down and enjoy the life God had for them. But before entering the Promised Land, they wanted to be sure the present landowners wouldn't put up too much of a fight. Moses sent 12 leaders to spy out the land of their dreams. Ten of the 12 became dream breakers. They saw the land overflowing with abundance but warned that they couldn't go in because the present occupants were HUGE. In comparison to these giants, the people of Israel were like grasshoppers. The other two spies, Joshua and Caleb, said the land was filled with an abundance of every good thing, and as long as the Lord was with them, they could defeat the giants and possess the land. Caleb and Joshua were ready to make the dream a reality.

Who did the children of Israel listen to? The dream breakers! Fear, negativity and the inability to see God's provision and power prevailed. As a result, the people lived in the wilderness for 40 years until a new generation decided to believe in God the dream maker. Only then did they possess the land.

Who are you listening to? Are you leading with a vision that God gave you, or with fear of possibilities? Are you a dream maker or a dream breaker? If a curse or a blessing is to come to pass in your life, your agreement is required.

Your Past Does Not Determine Your Destination

Dream breakers struggle with letting go of the past instead of embracing the future. It's good to remember the past but not live in it. New dreams are waiting to come into focus, but they can be blocked by past disappointments, negative words and past hurts. Life-altering moments can be a breakthrough or a breakdown. Never let a past mistake stop you from moving forward. The breakthrough happens when you make the change. One of the key things I convey to leaders is that their past does not determine their final destination. Don't dig up things God has already forgotten. Every leader that comes in to Lakewood knows there is a clean slate where they can write whatever dream they have on the chalkboard. The future is too important to live in the past.

Moving Toward Glory, Not Back to It

Sometimes it's not a negative past that breaks our dreams, but rather a desire to relive the glory days instead of going from glory to glory. We can stop dreaming and start complaining: "I remember when it used to be good." "This will never happen." "I wish we could bring back the good old days." There is nothing wrong with the good old days, but your best days are not behind you; they are in front of you no matter how old you are. Growing old never stops the one with a young heart who understands that each dream can carry him or her into a new adventure.

A dear friend and great woman of faith named Dawn dreamed for years of having children. God had promised her that she was going to not only have children, but that she was going to have a set of twins—a boy and a girl. As the years went by, it seemed like the dream was unlikely. She reached the age where most people don't consider having children. Yet Dawn knew that time was not a factor with a God who is timeless. She shared her dream with everyone she met. I'm sure people were asking if she really wanted to have children in her fifties.

She could have been hurt that God hadn't given her children when she was younger, but instead of focusing on the past, she embraced the future promise that someday her dream would happen. She had a room in her house waiting for their arrival for seven years. When others would be relaxing and enjoying life, Dawn was getting ready for her biggest adventure.

For 21 years she held on to her dream. At just past 50 years of age, Dawn became pregnant with twins: a boy and a girl. She did not let age or the past steal her future dreams. Her kids are happy and healthy, and mom and dad couldn't be prouder.

Do not let the dream breakers tell you it's too late or it will never happen. No one can stop a dream that God has already birthed. Only *we* can break the dreams of our own lives by doubting what God has already promised us. Rick Warren says, "When God gives a principle, He gives a promise." I always say, "If you believe in the principle, you can count on the promise." I heard a great quote the other day: "We can either surrender to the opposition we face in our lives, or we can surrender to a cause—a mission so great that the opposition doesn't matter. It only serves to help us focus." Pastor Joel says, "God can take that stumbling block and make it your stepping stone."

Looking Up from the Trenches

Robin Chandler
Lakewood Team Member

Throughout my life, particularly during my collegiate and professional career, I have known some exceptional and effective leaders. Yet it is Pastor Craig Johnson who has had a significant influence on me, as I understand the importance of vertical leadership. Craig has taught his team that the most important job a leader has is to "build and inspire people." Human beings are the most valued resource in ministry, business and family. Pastor Craig has always said, "A leader never gives up on people," and he stresses the need to start in love. He has challenged me to focus on who I am leading, and not on myself, because God has a greater purpose for me that is bigger than myself.

Pastor Craig demonstrates his faith and confidence in the leaders he has developed by allowing them to become all that God has created them to be. Most human behavior, positive or negative, is learned from those you spend the most time with. In order to build strong teams, vertical leaders must model by their example, which should be based on their desire to fulfill God's purpose.

Pastor Craig's teachings on the skills needed by effective leaders have been the tools I have used as I lead in family situations, ministry and personal relationships. Leadership begins with "me and my life," and I must use my witness, experiences and lessons learned as an example to follow. Craig has said that "Leadership begins with me and my life . . . my example is the greatest leadership tool." I've used this principle in teaching my own children to embrace the gifts and talents God has placed in them.

I have an eighth-grade student who has natural leadership tendencies but is learning how to be a model, living out his beliefs for others to see. I have helped my son understand that leaders, no matter their age, have to take responsibility for and be accountable for their actions. My son is a leader when he sets a godly example for his peers. He has been in some uncomfortable situations where many kids would have compromised their integrity to be with the "in crowd." However, my son has chosen to excuse himself and continues to model godly behavior, which I believe is because of the principles he has learned from Pastor Craig's teachings.

Jesus Christ, who is our Shepherd, modeled leadership and is the ultimate example of an effective leader. In parallel, Pastor Craig exemplifies the type of leader that Jesus was on earth, and he is committed to encouraging the leaders he serves to rely on God to build their ministries and homes. He has appealed to his team to rise above circumstances and take their lives to new levels in godly leadership, no matter how great the obstacles faced.

QUESTIONS FOR ACTION

1. Identify dream breakers who have had a negative impact on your life. What or who has given them the power to have that impact?

2. What causes good people to become dream breakers?

3. How will drawing near to God help you restore dreams where they've already been broken in your organization?

4. When have you received "constructive criticism"? How did your relationship with that person make a difference in how you received his or her words?

5. In what ways have you experienced this truth: Your focus will determine what you listen to?

6. Are you more concerned with pleasing dream breakers or pleasing God who loves you deeply? Why?

7. In what ways has your past hindered you in the pursuit of your dreams?

8. Reflect on how you have unintentionally broken the dreams of those on your team, and then take some steps to restore their dreams.

Note

  1. Jonathan Foreman and Timothy Foreman, "We Were Meant to Live" (Brentwood, TN: EMI Christian Music Group, 2003).

7

The Goal Is Never More Important than the Person

Don't build a dam in front of what needs to be poured out of your life for someone else. To truly lead another life, one must be willing to give up a part of one's own.

My first year at Lakewood our team's mission centered on moving into the Compaq Center and preparing for the large increase of children we believed were headed our way. We had to work fast to move into the children's facility, develop programs, recruit volunteers and model new areas of ministry.

In the midst of that blur of activity we held two large outreach gatherings: an event with Veggie Tales and another with Wacky World creator Bruce Barry. Before we knew it, the grand opening had arrived, and we got slammed. My excitement and enthusiasm preparing for the launch (which was outstanding) blinded me to the pace our team had maintained for months. Our passion for excellence took its toll on our entire team of staff and volunteers. We were accomplishing goals and building team members up to do the ministry, but we were not building team members up to persevere through the ministry. The goal became more important than the people. If I didn't take my foot off the gas, I was going to run over the most important people God had given me.

When your passion punishes your team, it's time to reevaluate priorities. When your drive comes at the expense of the people who helped you get there, you must ask whether you are pushing for the sake of building into people's lives or to further your desire to accomplish great things. I have found that when God wants to move, it has nothing to do with urgency; it has to do with timing. We think we have to do it now or it won't get done. We tell ourselves that if we miss the window of opportunity, the door will close forever. We feel constrained by the tyranny of our passion (a close cousin to the tyranny of the urgent). Our passion for our program blinds us to the effect we are having on others. In other words, things that seemed urgent at the time might not seem like a big deal in a few weeks. Are we driving our teams in the name of reckless passion? Have we produced results but not counted the cost of those who were hurt to get the results we wanted?

In his book *Integrity*, Henry Cloud describes a time when he sat on the aft deck of a ship watching the wake. He wrote that you can tell a lot about a ship by looking at its wake. If the wake is a straight line, the boat is on course. But if it's wavering, you begin to wonder about the stability of the ship.[1] When we focus solely on the goal and not on the impact on the team, we can leave a lot of our team members in our wake. Yet, if we build the person as we pursue the goal, no one will drown in our wake. What does your wake look like? Don't let passion kill the people you should be most passionate about . . . your team.

Driving Lessons

Have you ever been late to a meeting and decided to speed through traffic, only to stop at the next red light and notice that in the next lane over is one of the cars you so urgently passed awhile back? Speeding does not guarantee that you'll get there faster! Speed may not get you there faster, but knowledge will. If you know the right road to take, understand where traffic is the heaviest and prepare ahead of time, you can almost always get there right on time. When you take time to reflect and plan your day according to what's best for the program *and* the team, you will experience more growth than you ever imagined.

Have you ever made a sharp turn and driven your front wheel up on the curb and have it drop back down onto the road with a bang? At first it seems like the car is fine, but soon you notice a slight pull to the left. As long as you keep your hands on the wheel it seems fine. Six months pass and that slight pull is beginning to make the steering wheel shake. *It's not that bad,* you think. *I can still drive the car.* Months later your tires are worn, the wheel bearings are just about shot, the front end shakes and if you let go of the wheel your car veers sharply to the left. When the wheels are out of alignment, it always gets worse.

I've seen many leaders work this way. They are good people who have had success, but somewhere along the line their focus shifts, like a car going out of alignment. They begin to compromise their core purpose or belief. Ever so slightly they begin to entertain ideas that shift the company in a self-serving direction. At one time it was about building the team, but now it is about building themselves. They want success so badly that they forget to focus on the core values that got them there. It's important to continue to ask, "Why do we do the things we do?"

I've been honored to spend time with many leaders across the country and encourage them to explore why they do what they do. In one meeting, I asked a group of talented and effective leaders why they used a certain component of their program. What were they hoping to accomplish? A bit surprised by the question, the only answer they could give was that they thought it was cool and other people would think it was cool too. "Well that's great," I said, "but why do you do it? What is the message behind your program? The cool factor will wear out if there is no principle. The message is what keeps it in alignment."

To stay in alignment, we have to continually ask three questions: (1) Why do we do what we do? (2) Where do we want to take people? (3) Does what we do line up with our core principles? A vertical leader is not afraid of the questions, because the answers are already established.

When I came to Lakewood, I did not build the children's ministry based on what had been done at other churches. I looked to see what Lakewood was about and built on those core values. Pastor Joel is a pastor of hope, so everything we did was going to communicate hope. Lakewood is a church with an overwhelming sense of love, so we made sure when we built teams or welcomed families that they would feel loved. Lakewood has incredible worship music, so one of the first things I worked on at Kidslife was building strong praise and worship teams.

Today we have more than 15 different worship teams leading multiple services. We believe in people, no matter where they come from or what they've been through. So all of our leaders speak words like "I believe in you," "Your best days are ahead of you" and "If you can dream it, we will help you build it." All of these core values were already a part of who we were, and they continue to keep us in alignment.

Take Out the Trash

I love conferences and books, but I see too many leaders following a conference instead of a vision. They take the latest idea from the latest conference and end up acting like a fast-food restaurant that produces whatever they think might sell. Maybe our ministries don't grow the way we want them to because we've piled up too many ideas and we can't see anything over the pile!

Have you ever seen one of those television shows that feature people who behave like pack rats? They buy so much stuff, and it gets piled up so high that they can't see out the windows of their house. The things they really need, like the furniture, counter space and washer and dryer, are hidden by the piles of stuff. All they really needed was what they already had.

Sometimes we get so overwhelmed by new ideas that we don't have any room for what we really need: God ideas. God has gifted every leader with key abilities and vision that no one else can carry out. You get out of alignment when you start doing other people's vision instead of finding the vision that God has already planted in you.

We also get out of alignment when we chase things that in the long run don't really matter. Rather than impacting and building people, we end up doing things that are frivolous. We lose focus when we fritter our time on busywork instead of productive work. I've heard it said that sometimes we just have to take out the trash! The trash is anything that keeps us from the only thing that matters. The goal is never more important than the person: Invest in people.

Dr. Paul Osteen has been a great influence on my life. I've never met anyone who cares for the hurting and broken like he does. Through his example, I've learned that what you do for yourself will never mean as much as what you do for others. I've watched him walk into a room and make sure everyone else matters except him. His compassion for people compels others to be the hands and feet of hope to a hurting world. Why does he respond this way? Because he knows the goal is never more important than the person.

The apple doesn't fall too far from the tree. Momma Dodie Osteen is an example who so many of us try to emulate. She cares for others like an angel of mercy. At 76 years young, she is a hospital to the hurting. One year she sent more than 16,000 handwritten notes to encourage people. She leads a weekly prayer service at Hermann Memorial Hospital as well as a prayer and healing time every Tuesday night at Lakewood. A friend wrote a post on her Facebook page about her mother-in-law's cancer and upcoming chemotherapy. She wanted everybody to pray for her mother-in-law. I told her I would pray and also call Miss Dodie, who is a cancer overcomer, to pray for her as well. Vertical leaders aren't survivors; they are overcomers. Miss Dodie not only prayed for her, but she also called her personally the day before the chemotherapy. Kathleen said her mother-in-law's countenance changed in an instant. Instead of thinking about what she was going to go through, she began to think about how her new friend Dodie cared enough about her to call and lift her spirits. That is a vertical leader moment! Miss Dodie knows that the goal is never more important than the person.

What Can Happen When the Goal Is More Important than the Person?

Have you ever had a best friend, someone you connected with right away? Larry was that kind of friend for me. I had come to Long Beach City College in Long Beach, California, with a lot of goals. My family had been telling me that I had a calling to be a minister, but that was the last thing I wanted when I graduated from high school. I wanted to be a public servant: a mayor, then a congressman, then a senator or governor. I had a passion to serve people, but I didn't see ministers as successful. The ministers I knew didn't seem to impact the world the way I wanted to. How much of a difference could just working in a local church make? I wanted to serve God, but not as a pastor. I wanted to make money, and pastors didn't make money; they gave it away. I wanted to be a power broker, a world changer and a history maker. Did you notice a lot of *I*s in my sentences?

When I came to Long Beach, I got involved right away in a service fraternity, meeting Larry the night I pledged. Larry was one of the nicest guys I had ever met. It seemed like he had it all; he had big goals, and we hit it off right away. We ended up sharing a house together with some other friends. Larry and I both got more involved in our fraternity. I became the fraternity president and then the Associated Men's Student President at LBCC. I was doing the things I set out to do; my goals were being met and life could not be better.

I was not only taking classes and being active on campus, but I was also managing a restaurant in Long Beach. Larry was working there as well. We did everything together, from school to working to sharing a house to intramural sports. We never seemed to get tired of hanging out together. We even gave each other dating advice, not that we always listened to each other! We acted like brothers, and over time, I began to fill the role of a big brother that Larry looked up to. Larry leaned on me as someone he thought he could depend on.

One night after our restaurant shift was over, Larry told me he was going to his parents' home to give his sister some insurance money for his car. I thought it was odd that he was taking the money home instead of paying his insurance himself, but I figured he had his reasons. It was ten o'clock when he left the restaurant, and I went home and fell asleep. At three o'clock that morning, I heard someone taking a shower. Rolling over, I tried to go back to sleep, but later heard dishes clanging in the kitchen. At four o'clock, I yelled from the bedroom, "Whoever is up, go to bed—I'm trying to sleep!" It got quiet until I heard Emergency Services coming down the street and stop in front of our house. It was about 7:00 in the morning when I walked into the living room and heard a fireman say, "He [Larry] doesn't want to wake up his friends." Larry was sitting on the end table next to the couch, his eyes dilated to the size of golf balls. The paramedic told me that Larry had called them because after taking cocaine, it felt like his body was tearing apart.

I asked if they were going to take Larry to the hospital, but they said they thought he was going to be okay; but it might be a good idea for me to take him to the ER just as a precaution. To this day, I still can't grasp why they asked me, someone with no medical experience, to drive him to the emergency room when they could have taken him. Reluctantly, I took Larry by the arm and walked him to my truck. Or at least I tried to walk him to my truck. He was so high that I had a hard time staying with him.

As we drove, he told me that he had lied about going to see his sister to give her the insurance money. Instead he had met up with some old friends to party. He revealed that he had been in a drug rehab before he came to Long Beach City College. He was trying to turn his life around by starting school. Yet, earlier that evening, he had snorted several lines of cocaine, which we later found out was laced with crystal meth.

I said, "Larry, why are you doing drugs? That stuff is messed up." He said, "I know, CJ, please don't tell our friends. This has got to stay between you and me." You see, even though Larry and I would drink at fraternity parties, we never went beyond that. Drugs were not a part of my game plan for life, and I had never thought they were part of Larry's. I was overwhelmed to realize that I had no clue whether this was his first relapse or if he had been keeping drug use hidden from me for a while. While I was trying to figure out how to get to the hospital, Larry said, "CJ, am I shaking?" I glanced over and said, "A little bit—hold on, we'll be at the hospital in a minute." He asked me again, "CJ, am I shaking?" I was getting scared because the shaking was getting stronger. Then Larry grabbed the front of the dashboard, crying out, "CJ, HELP ME!"

Breaking into violent convulsions, Larry's head and arms began to hit the dashboard and the window. It seemed like forever but was probably only a minute or so before it stopped and his chin dropped to his chest. I pulled his head back with one arm, and noticed his eyes roll back. I shook him and yelled his name. I had to keep driving because I was afraid he would die before we got to the hospital. After yelling his name a couple of times, I heard him mumble "CJ" very lightly. I'm not sure how we made it to the hospital, but I was so relieved to see the signs for the ER. I ran in to get the emergency staff, and when we got to the truck, Larry was still dazed. As we pulled him out of the car, he kept on mumbling, "CJ, where am I?"

Once we got into the emergency room, I could feel myself starting to calm down. Everything was going to be okay because we had made it to the hospital, and Larry was in good hands. Still shaken by what had happened, I headed home to pick up Larry's identification and a few other things and then I went directly back to the hospital.

What happened next has been seared into my memory. As I walked to the desk to give them Larry's ID, a nurse grabbed me and asked, "Is that your friend you brought in here?" I nodded. She said, "We lost him twice in the emergency room. He is in a coma on a ventilator. I want you to do something for me. I'm going to take you behind the partition to see your friend. I want you to tell your other friends what drugs can do. Too many kids lose their lives from a senseless act. I don't want to see any more of your friends die." As we went around the partition, I could not believe my eyes: my best friend lay in a coma, connected to what seemed like every machine in the hospital. My mind went numb, because I had thought everything was okay, but it wasn't.

Over the next few months, I watched Larry waste away from 180 pounds down to 90 pounds. I sat by his bedside, saying, "Larry, if you can hear me, Jesus loves you." I had heard that people in comas can hear you, even if they can't respond. I didn't know if Larry was a Christian or not, so I told him, "Larry, Jesus loves you. All you have to do is ask Him into your heart." In my spirit, I heard a voice speak to me, saying, "Craig, you had every opportunity to tell him about Me, but you never did. Don't let another friend go down without telling them the good news."

I could have led Larry to Christ at any moment. He trusted me. He would have followed my lead, but I never used the influence I had on his life. I was so zoned into what I wanted to accomplish and how I wanted to be successful that I never shared Christ with Larry.

I don't carry the responsibility for Larry's decisions or for his salvation. That is between Larry and God. What I felt God was saying to me was, "Craig, the goal is never more important than the person. Influence people positively, Craig, not negatively. Bring hope and life and notice those around you that you have influence over. Don't get so caught up in the program that you forget the person. Success isn't what you can obtain; success is who you can build."

There are different kinds of leaders, but I believe we can all be leaders. We can all think vertically. It's when we only use our own eyes, and don't look through God's, that a tragedy like the one I've just recounted can happen right under our noses.

Shortly after we buried Larry, I did the first drug and alcohol forum at Long Beach City College, with Larry's mom holding a picture of her son. We spoke to hundreds of students. Thousands of people, young and old, have been impacted by Larry's story. God was not blaming me for Larry. He was reminding me of the influence I could have on all the Larrys I would meet in the future. To the best of my ability, I have never let another friend go down without hearing the message of hope from my life. That's when I realized my true calling to help build leaders who can bring hope and restoration to kids and families through the local church. I've heard it said that sometimes you can meet your destiny on the road you take to avoid it.

When you get behind the wheel of your car with your children in the backseat, you're a role model—a leader. When you are in the office, you may think no one cares how you conduct yourself, but you're wrong, because you're a leader. When you go to school and live life with your friends, you're a leader. If you are the CEO of a multi-billion-dollar corporation, you are not just a moneymaker, you are a leader impacting lives. Don't build a dam in front of what needs to be poured out of your life into someone else's. To truly lead in another's life, you must be willing to give up a part of your own.

Looking Up from the Trenches

Ashlee Hurst
Lakewood Team Member

Under the leadership of Pastor Craig, I led a team of people on a large project at our church. I had two people under me who, while leading different portions of the project, also had to work together. They didn't get along, and I was constantly putting out fires between them. I found myself having to either choose sides or upset both of them. It was a difficult place to be, and I constantly struggled with what to do and how to bring peace to the team. One of the leaders developed a bad attitude and began saying hurtful things about the other person to the rest of the team. The other one wanted to quit and started missing some of our meetings.

I went before God on many occasions, seeking wisdom. It seemed that the more I tried to bring peace, the harder it became to find it. I wanted to cancel the project, but because of the hundreds of people involved, that was not an option.

During a talk with Pastor Craig, he told me to pray and seek God for wisdom, and search my heart to see if there was anything that I needed to change. My first thought was, *Are you kidding me? I have gone out of my way to try to make both of them happy. I have done everything I can think of to do.* But I was desperate. I didn't want to fail, and knew that the project would never be completed if something drastic didn't happen. It felt drastic to ask God what I could change, because I did not think I was doing anything wrong.

So, I went home, got on my knees and cried out to God to help me search my heart to see if I needed to change anything. I felt like He was telling me that I needed to humble myself and apologize to the volunteer with the bad attitude. I was totally confused. I thought, *Why do I have to apologize to this person? God, shouldn't she apologize to me? She is the one causing division here, not me!* I felt that God was saying, "If you want peace, then humble yourself before her."

About an hour later, I called her on the phone and apologized. I told her I was sorry if there was anything that I had done to make her feel that her job was not important or if it seemed like I was showing favoritism to the other leader. I told her how important she was to the team and how much I appreciated what she did.

Her response was totally unexpected. At first she was speechless, and then she said, "Thank you. I have been waiting for and needed to hear you say those words for weeks." I couldn't believe it. She had felt left out. She didn't think that I wanted her on the team or needed her. And after thinking about everything we had gone through, I realized there were times that I favored the other leader.

I realized that I had put the goal of accomplishing the project ahead of the person. I knew that I had not encouraged and supported her the way a leader should. I was the one in the wrong. I did need to humble myself and apologize.

At our next meeting, it was like having a new team. There was a peace in the room. Everything fell into place perfectly; finally there was unity! And it all happened because I humbled myself and realized that I was putting the goal ahead of my team.

The project ended up being a huge success. We received letters and praise from our entire church. Many lives were touched and many people saved. It was a life-changing experience for everyone involved.

I am so grateful for Pastor Craig's advice. I will never do another project without making sure that I am putting my team ahead of the goal. And I will never be reluctant again to humble myself and do whatever God is asking me to do. James 4:10 says, "Humble yourselves before the Lord, and he will lift you up." I felt that humbling myself not only lifted me up with honor, but my entire team was lifted up as well.

It was a very difficult experience to go through, but I learned a valuable lesson about leading a team. My perspective on what a leader is supposed to be has been changed. I now know that just reaching a goal does not mean you are successful; the process of leading the team is just as important and can bring even greater success. What good is reaching a goal if people are hurt and treated poorly in the process? With everything I do now, I ask God what I can change about myself as a leader to make my team more successful. I am always checking my heart and motives to make sure that my God and my team are the first priority, not the goal.

QUESTIONS FOR ACTION

1. Describe a time when the tyranny of your passion blinded you from the impact you had on others.

2. Reflect on how you've led your team over the past year by answering the three questions of alignment: (1) Why do you do what you do? (2) Where do you want to take people? (3) Does what you do line up with your core principles?

3. What "trash" prevents you from understanding God's vision for you as a leader of your organization?

4. In what ways do you relate to my relationship with Larry at school? In what ways do you relate to what God was teaching me in Larry's death?

5. Make a list of the important people that have been placed in your life. Decide if you've placed your personal goals above having a positive influence in each of their lives.

Note

1. Dr. Henry Cloud, *Integrity: The Courage to Meet the Demands of Reality* (New York: Harper-Business, 2006), p. 18.

8

Reputations 'R' Us

Fulfillment in life cannot be grasped by building things;
it can only be obtained by building people.

Marcos Witt, one of the most incredible leaders I know, spoke to a group of youth leaders, saying, "Everyone needs to be affirmed. Affirmation is giving a person a reputation to live up to."[1] When we affirm people, we lay the groundwork for them to become their best selves. We give them a reputation that will inspire them to reach higher than where they were standing. Our words help others see themselves from a different perspective. Authentic affirmation also helps us receive life's greatest reward: having a positive impact on the life of another. The reward in life is not looking back to see how much you've accomplished but rather in seeing how many people you have built up along the way. When you affirm, inspire, and build up people, you will accomplish more than you could have ever done on your own.

In order to build reputation, Marcos calls leaders to become word craftsmen who paint pictures of hope. What kind of pictures are you painting? Is your canvas of encouragement blank? Let's pick up a paintbrush and look at multiple ways to encourage others to reach their goals.

The First Stroke:
Choose Your 12 and Affirm

Our staff writes cards of encouragement twice a year to every team member. These are not generic thank-you notes but well-thought-out cards specific to each person. You need to know your team before you can speak into the lives of your team. We have more than 1,250 volunteers in Kidslife. I may not know all of my team personally, but someone on my staff does! This is the power of building disciples. While Jesus spoke to thousands, He heavily invested in 12. This ancient model of a rabbi investing in the life of a small number of students is one of the greatest leadership models ever given. Jesus' disciples were not simply men who followed Him; they were His leadership team in training. It's important that the team you personally build is not too big. Choose your 12 and go deep. At the same time, you'll also build into the larger group in your organization, but at a different level.

Leaders often mistakenly try to build the corporate group before building the small group. To be effective, Jesus knew He could go deep with a smaller group and still speak to the corporate crowd. He knew the "in-depth team" would branch off and multiply, going house to house to build the corporate group.

When I'm working on the cards of encouragement, I only send them to my small group of about 20. It takes me an entire day to write them because I know that personal words of encouragement have to be specific. My team knows that I know what they are working on and the impact that it's making.

Have you ever met a leader who feels like the thrill is gone or the honeymoon is over? Many times it's because they don't realize the impact of their faithful service. These cards of encouragement can change the grind of doing the job into a grand opportunity to do the job only they can do. Sure, others could do the job, but God didn't give you others; He gave you this team.

I love the scene from the movie *Hoosiers* where the star player has chosen not to play for the team. As the team comes out on the court to be introduced at the pep rally, the fans begin to chant the star player's name. The coach says, "I would hope you would support who we are, not who we are not. These six individuals have made a choice to work, a choice to sacrifice and put themselves on the line to represent you. That kind of commitment and effort deserves and demands your respect. This is your team!"

It is great to project and gauge where you are and where you want to be, but leaders make a mistake when they don't take time to identify what they already have. There is a difference between picking teams and building teams. You don't always get to pick your team. Your choice is to either build the team you've been given or complain about how you don't have the team you should have. Remember, this is your team. Start there. Support who you are, not who you are not.

I not only write cards, but I also send multiple emails to recognize a job well done or as encouragement while they are working on a project. We remember birthdays with cards and parties to celebrate their day. We give what we call "take homes." These are usually some kind of object lesson or faith objective to help them build their personal life. The dream cards are one example of a "take home" that we might give. Another example would be when we gave parents a large Kidslife coin to carry wherever they went to remind them of the value of their family. We have written monthly devotionals for our staff about issues leaders go through in everyday life. We make these available both on our website and on CDs so they can listen in the car.

The Second Stroke:
Verbal Words of Encouragement

Verbal encouragement is most powerful when it is authentic and consistent. You can't be an in-'n'-out encourager. Some leaders will only speak into people's lives at the big moments. They are only looking at the Super Bowl moments, not the practice times that get you to the big game. Sometimes we're so busy looking for the big things in life that we forget that the little moments count. A quarterback has to slow down the action on the field to make sure he makes an accurate pass. Great leaders value the opportunities that most leaders will miss. What others may view as insignificant, vertical leaders see as essential.

It is hard for me to touch base with all of our paid staff and volunteer team all the time. What I do, though, is walk through Kidslife and the youth department every week to say hello and encourage my team so that I can make a connection with them on a consistent basis. Do I have to do it? Not necessarily. But what a huge difference it can make to do what you don't have to do. Team builders teach their team through example. If I'm in my office, my leaders will stay in their offices. If I'm on the floor connecting with my team, my leaders will be on the floor connecting with their team. Ralph Waldo Emerson said, "What you do shouts so loudly in my ears, I cannot hear what you say."

Pastor Joel and Victoria greet every visitor after every service at Lakewood. I've never seen any pastor care more for the newcomer than Joel. Many people come from all over the world to visit Lakewood, and Joel doesn't want to let them down. If they take the time to come, Joel and Victoria will take the time to say hello. They could be back in their offices preparing for the next service, but instead the Osteens will personally greet the hundreds of people who line up after every service. It makes a huge impression on the visitors, just as it makes a huge impression on your team when you do the extra work to connect with them individually. The following are some of the different ideas we use consistently to build our teams.

Weekly Devotionals and Staff Meetings
We used to hold two-hour staff meetings where only one or two people did the talking. I would watch my team come out of those

meetings looking drained instead of inspired. If all you talk about is business and tasks, even though there are exciting things going on, you feel drained.

God spoke to me one day, telling me that my number-one job as a leader was to build and inspire the people I lead. Let the business flow out of the spiritual instead of expecting the spiritual to flow out of the business. It will change your team. So instead of doing two-hour staff meetings talking about business, we started each meeting with 15 minutes of prayer and worship. We incorporated an accountability time where people could pair off to share a personal need, a ministry need and a praise report. Every week I prepare a 30-minute devotional just for our team, to speak encouragement to them. The meeting is built around inspiring them to rise higher. Then we take 45 minutes to work on business.

This new format has revolutionized our staff meetings. While it once took two hours to discuss business, now it only takes 45 minutes. While I'm sure that in the past my leaders dreaded going to staff meetings, now most of the team says it's the number-one thing they look forward to every week. Why? Because business at times can weigh you down, but inspiration will lift you up. After they are inspired, they are ready to take on challenges with a different mindset.

Team Cheers

All throughout Kidslife you will see and hear multiple huddles and cheers. The cheers are creative and distinctive to each group and provide a sense of team spirit that gets them ready to take on the world. Every team does its own cheer after their small-group time. You might say, "Craig, that is corny, I'm an adult, not a high school kid." While you may be an adult, you're also a part of a team, and teams cheer each other on. If you don't give your team a model or tools to use to cheer each other on, they will find something else to cheer for. The more you cheer, the more people will hear. Cheering people on draws a crowd, but a critic usually stands alone. Become your team's biggest fan!

Small Groups

Every service for every grade in Kidslife has a small-group time every week. The leaders provide all these small-group times to encourage their teams and clearly communicate upcoming vision and direction for Kidslife. They are also great times to pray and cheer each other on. We have more than 150 ministry small groups just in Kidslife. If you oversee a division in your business and break it down by departments, you could have a small group with your department leaders, and your department leaders would have a small-group time with their team leaders, and so on.

Large Team Meetings

Our quarterly team meetings are designed specifically for the volunteers and leaders, to inspire them to rise higher. They are themed with programming that honors our leaders for the outstanding acts of service they do every week.

Leadership Conferences

While we encourage our leaders to go to some of the great leadership conferences available, we found that it was difficult taking some and leaving out others who really needed it. We began planning our own leadership conferences for staff and volunteers here at Lakewood. Our conferences are free and feature leaders from our own teams as well as outside speakers. We are able to give our leaders an opportunity to grow, with many different classes to choose from. If you have a business or church, you can do the same thing no matter what the size. You might be surprised at how many people within your organization have skills or leadership training to offer. Our "Keys Conference" has been instrumental in taking our leaders to the next level.

The Third Stroke:
Gifts of Encouragement

These are gifts of encouragement that show the gratitude and appreciation we feel toward every volunteer or staff member who works so hard on our team.

Gift Cards

Every once in a while, I might buy five-dollar Blockbuster or Starbucks gift cards that just say thank-you in a small way, from our heart to yours. You will be amazed at how a small gift card can encourage one of your leaders. It's the thought that you cared enough to take time to do something for them. They love it! At our last team meeting of the year, we have a big "thank-you giveaway." Each staff member either buys or gets a few gifts donated and we have a huge night honoring our team, raffling off gifts for the volunteer team members. It's an amazing night that inspires so many people.

Team Awards

At quarterly team meetings, each staff member chooses an outstanding volunteer who has done extraordinary work serving the ministry. We announce these "star awards" in front of the whole team and give them a certificate to the Lakewood Bookstore. They are truly honored, and it's great to watch the team they serve with cheer them on for their accomplishments.

Acts of Service

Over the years, we have performed a variety of acts of service for team members: We have sent teams to help staff members move, clean their homes after a hurricane and bring food when someone is sick or in bereavement. We plan baby showers and birthday parties for volunteers and staff. Perhaps one of the biggest things our church provides is free childcare for our staff through the workweek and free ministry event childcare in the evenings. This allows volunteers and staff to participate in church events and blesses them financially as well.

The Fourth Stroke: Gift of Training and Development

We provide multiple levels of training to all our staff members. "Basic training" prepares each new volunteer leader to begin service in Kidslife. "Raise the Bar" training not only helps volunteers grow in their department but also develops leadership skills for whatever area they choose to advance into at Kidslife. "Star training" teaches spirituality, teamwork, ambassadorship and responsibility (safety). After completing the four modules, a person becomes a Kidslife STAR certified team member.

We also developed three leadership training levels for every age group, beginning in third grade. J-Life is a curriculum mentorship program that develops kids in multiple areas of leadership and the arts. We graduate more than 150 kids a year. Teen-life, a leadership program for seventh-grade students through twelfth-grade students, provides opportunities to serve and develop leadership skills and trains more than 250 young people who serve in Kidslife. Finally, the Lakewood Internship Program is a nine-month program of leadership classes, development in multiple ministries and training for adults, whether they want to raise their leadership in the marketplace or go into full- or part-time ministry. We have 25 to 30 interns serving in multiple departments every year.

Build the People; Build the Organization

Kidslife is a success not because of the church in which we're located, the programs we put on or the building we occupy. Kidslife is a success because of the God we serve and the people we build to serve others. If you build the people, you will build the organization. The goal can never be more important than the person, because the person helps you reach the goal.

Looking Up from the Trenches

Shawna Collins
Lakewood Volunteer

One of the most important things I have learned from Pastor Craig is that *leadership* is simply *influence*. Influence is the act of producing an effect without directly commanding. Wow, so if I influence people, I lead them? I have used this concept at work and at home, teaching my children that they are leaders when they influence others. Will they use their leadership skills to influence someone the right way?

Just because we are leaders at heart doesn't make us good leaders! Pastor Craig taught me that if I was to be a good leader, I needed to influence the situation, not let the situation influence me. Although I have been in leadership roles in my career for the past six years, I never thought about it that way. I assumed that I was a natural leader and that I just have what it takes, right? How wrong I was all of those years! I have taken this concept learned from Pastor Craig and incorporated it into all of my relationships. If there is an opportunity for me to influence someone, there is an opportunity for me to *lead* someone on the right path!

The foundation of leadership is relationships. People will not go along with you if they don't get along with you (another Pastor Craig teaching). No matter how busy we are, we need to make time for others. Great leaders value people and make themselves available. During my internship, Pastor Craig asked the interns to send him an email each week telling of one act of kindness we did for someone in our life. It sounded like an easy task, but I really had to intentionally find someone to be good to! I loved the concept so much that I incorporated it at work with my employees, and it has created a lot of positive energy. My employees work in different locations, so I decided to take it a step further and let *them* know how much I value them! I sent out thank-you notes to their homes, and people started telling other departments how much it meant to them. We incorporated the policy throughout our entire organization of 4,000 employees, and now there are a lot more people in this world who feel a little more valuable!

The leadership training I have received from Pastor Craig has been invaluable, especially his teaching on character and integrity. Titus 2:7-8 says, "Be an example to them by doing good works of every kind. Let everything you do reflect the integrity and seriousness of your teaching. Let your teaching be so correct that it can't be criticized" (*NLT*). Your skills may take you far, but your character will keep you there.

When I am making tough hiring decisions, I have learned that I can teach certain job duties to people, but character is something I should look for, because it is not something I can teach. Character and integrity are the most important qualities I look for in any relationship I have, work or personal. I have incorporated integrity into just about every meeting or decision our senior leadership team makes within our company. My boss now tells our clients that I keep him in line if he starts doing anything that would jeopardize our integrity.

One day, after meeting with some potential clients (in which we discussed one of our values—integrity!), they were following us to a restaurant for dinner. My boss was about to make a U-turn where it clearly said NO U-TURN, and I quickly called out in a joking manner, "Hey, is that showing integrity?" He didn't make the U-turn, and he still laughs about me taking our value of integrity *very* seriously.

If we are faithful to God in every aspect of our life, big or small, He will be faithful to us and trust us with so much more!

We need to tie all of these principles together by seeking God through prayer and through His Word. As we stay in prayer, we should always check our hearts to ensure that all of the glory and honor are going to God. Pastor Craig is a great example to me of a servant leader who shows humility while leading others. He has taught me that everyone has potential and needs to feel like they have accomplished something and made an impact. As leaders, we must stay in alignment and stay focused on the people in our lives!

QUESTIONS FOR ACTION

1. Affirmation is giving a person a reputation to live up to. Describe a time when someone affirmed you and inspired you to pursue a new direction.

2. Clearly identify which individuals in your organization are your "12." Write a personal note of affirmation to each of these individuals.

3. Of the different ideas for verbal encouragement listed below, which do you plan to implement into your leadership team:

- Walking around each week to speak words of affirmation to team members
- Intentionally getting to know visitors or new customers
- Weekly devotions
- Team cheers
- Small groups
- Large team meetings
- In-house leadership conferences

4. What gifts of encouragement could you easily give to your team members? What impact would that have on your team?

5. Evaluate the amount and quality of training offered to your team. What will you add in the future to affirm your team?

Note
1. Marcos Witt, speech delivered June 2009 at Lakewood Church.

9

The Money Fish

*Vertical leaders never look down, because they
cannot see what is ahead; will not just look forward,
because they can only see so far; but will always look up,
because they know God has the best view.*

Competitive bass fishing started right here in Texas, and now
has a big money tour with a top prize of $500,000. I don't
know about you, but I've never thought of fishing as a spectator
sport. You could wait all day for someone to catch just one fish.
But in fishing tournaments, fishermen are given a specific
amount of time to catch up to five fish. When they dock, each
fish is weighed. The competitor bringing in the highest combined
weight wins the big money. Those fish are considered the "money
fish." When I asked one fisherman what happens if you don't
catch anything, he laughed, saying, "If you know where to fish,
have the right lures and are persistent, you usually come back
with something. But if you want the 'money fish,' you have to
find the right spot."

In Luke chapter 5, Simon and his brother were fishing at Lake
Gennesaret while Jesus was preaching to a crowd on the shore.
Seeing that they hadn't caught any fish, Jesus got in the boat and
told them to pull away from the shore. Time for some tournament
fishing! Turning to Simon, Jesus said, "Throw out into the deep
water, and let down your nets for a catch." Simon argued, "Master, we have worked all night and have not caught any fish." Jesus
knew that if you find the right spot, have the right lures and are

persistent, you can catch a lot of fish. Simon and his companions threw out their nets and caught so many fish their nets could not hold them all. Those of us trying to build leadership teams should take notice. There are three keys to fishing for team members: (1) know where to fish, (2) have the right lure, (3) be persistent.

Know Where to Fish

For many churches across the country, paid staff members are a luxury. Most churches hire staff to fill a few key positions and then build a volunteer base. During my time at Faith Community Church, we had a large congregation and nearly 2,000 kids to serve, with only two full-time and two part-time staff. Our leadership team had to be volunteer-based, yet I needed high-impact eagles who could take the program to the next level. With so much to do and few resources at hand, vertical leaders have to prioritize and become solution oriented. Building teams rarely becomes a priority though, because it is perceived as such a tough, time-consuming job. Yet over the long term, without a team, it proves impossible to meet the needs of the church and help it grow. Far too much time is spent maintaining the church rather than building it. Ministering to individuals may be the ultimate goal of your church, but it isn't the most important thing for you to do. Why? You cannot possibly minister to them all by yourself. Your team will make or break your growth.

It's the same in business. We focus on sales because that's where the money comes from, when we should be focusing on building the sales team! I understand that we have to sell while we build, but our priority must be to build. The great leaders in history didn't do it alone.

So, if you cannot afford to hire a staff, where do you find your team? Have you ever gone fishing and seen 20 boats in the same area? With so many boats, how many fish do you think will be left? Many ministries and businesses fish in the same pond. Their volunteers have multiple hooks in their mouths; they serve in multiple ministries. It takes a vertical leader to ask God to show them a new pond. We need to fish in the pond that only God can see with His Google Earth perspective.

Will God really show us where we need to fish? Every time I have entered a new leadership situation, it has been different; and yet every time, I have known where to fish for leaders. Each time I have thought unconventionally, because I knew God was not going to do something common. I knew God was going to show me a different way of doing things. You might think, *If I could only get the pastor to make an announcement, then I would get the volunteers I need.* The question is not whether you will get the volunteers but whether you will get the right volunteers you need.

God never gives a leader an easy task. We were challenged with a hard task: building a team without hiring any staff. How could we find volunteers who could give the hours needed to truly elevate the ministry? We couldn't just fish in the same pond with everyone else; we needed to find a new pond! I had to trust God to show me where to find the big fish. In children's ministry, we usually look for educators, moms or anyone who's breathing. This time, though, we needed vertical leaders who could build people, develop ministry and move a vision. I needed a staff without paying a staff.

God led me to look for people who had never thought of serving in a kid's ministry. One thing I have learned is there is nothing predictable about God's choice. No elementary teachers and no super moms. Yet these were the people I was around all the time, the ones I thought had an affinity for children's ministry. But God was calling me to look further.

It may be shocking to think that you don't have to recruit people who have an affinity for your area of ministry. While you don't want to recruit people for a children's ministry who hate kids, you also don't have to bring on only those who are passionate about kids either. I know that may be hard for children's leaders to wrap their minds around, but remember, everyone is trying to fish from the same pond. Who says that a person who never had a desire to work with kids before could not work in children's ministry? I needed people to build the adults, not just the kids. We were building a church within a church that would provide multiple opportunities for people to serve in kids' and family ministry. Who says you have to have just singles working in a singles ministry? Can't a married couple lead a group? We were going to build something that would transcend one department, connect with other ministries and provide people with a variety of gifts and opportunity to serve.

At first I was skeptical about fishing in a new pond. After all, I was used to working with people who had a passion for kids. I realized that I needed to break out of the box. When you hang out with new people, you get a new perspective. So I was heading into uncharted territory, looking for a new pond to fish in, looking for the ones who were going to help build the future.

As I walked into the church gym one day, I noticed a lady sitting with books and a computer, working on the floor in the hallway. She had set up an office in the hallway while her kids were attending one of our programs. I had seen her many times before but had never really stopped to talk. Yet this time, because I had a new fishing pole, I stopped to ask her name. We started talking, and I learned that she brought her kids to multiple events. So I knew she was dedicated. She went on to tell me that she was the vice president of the largest independent bookstores in Southern California, and she was working while her kids were at our programs. That told me she could multi-task. I said, "Wow, you must be tired with running the kids to different places and the responsibility of your job." She said, "No, not really, I am actually doing really well." Now I knew she was high capacity. Then the most important question: Had she ever worked in children's ministry before? No, she had never really thought about it. Bingo! I knew I had caught my first money fish. She was exactly where God told me she would be.

Remember, Jesus told Simon to throw the net on the other side of the boat: He was saying, "Quit fishing where you know to fish and start fishing where I know you will catch fish." Vertical leadership challenges you to change the way you recruit and build people. Karen became a catalyst in building Kidznet at Faith Community Church. She, at times, volunteered 20 to 30 hours a week on top of everything else she did. She gave more than any staff member I could have paid. She was a money fish, a prize catch that only God could see.

Using the Right Lure

When you are trying to build something, you usually start at the bottom. It's tough to attract high-capacity leaders when you are at the bottom. When you have no reputation of success, most "money fish" never even hear of you; that's a tough place to start. You need to speak your vision into being, but the vision has to be followed by results. People want to be a part of something that is moving. If you are all hype, you'll end up like a cruise ship at the dock telling people it's leaving, but it never leaves port. There might be a great bon voyage celebration, but as soon as the passengers notice the ship isn't moving, they will leave. People follow passion, but they stay for results.

You have to believe in your excellence before you become excellent. It is not reality yet, but God has given you a dream. People follow dreams and vision because they feel like they are going somewhere. You need to use the right lure: a vision.

My goal is never to create a ministry but to ignite a movement. When you are building teams, you are not asking them to be a part of another ministry; you are asking them to be a part of a one-of-a-kind movement. If future team members are willing to catch the vision (or board the ship), we need to prepare them for their journey. They need to put God first in their lives, learn how to accomplish their goals and build their faith at home by making their first church their family. As a leader I try to find out about their troubles as well as their dreams. As a leader I want them to know that if they join the team, I will care about what is important to them. It's not just my vision; it's *our* vision.

Roxy Traughber was another person God gave me to build our team. Her children were almost grown, and she had never worked in children's ministry. Roxy had always worked in the music department, and I knew she was also an excellent administrator. One day while talking to her, God told me to throw the net out. Now, I knew that Roxy liked kids but never had a desire to work in that area. Even while presenting my vision I could tell she was not really interested. So I told her that this wasn't the stereotypical children's ministry. We were building departments in the ministry, and I needed someone to help develop bands, worship teams and kids' choirs to minister not only in Kidznet but also to the whole congregation. Now I had her attention! Developing kids to be true worshipers was a cause she could get behind. Yet, it wouldn't just be the kids. I told her I wanted family worship nights where kids and parents would worship together in the sanctuary.

It wasn't about her having to adapt to the vision; I begin to dream about the vision adapting to the leaders God was providing. Roxy went on to be the impetus of all things worship in Kidznet. She built multiple worship teams and headed up our Kidznet Family Worship Nights where 1,500 kids and parents would come together. She organized the first Kidznet-led worship night at a midweek service with a children's choir that she organized. Our pastor, Dr. Jim Reeve, told me it was one of the best nights of worship they'd had. She later came to Houston to help us launch Kidslife and now oversees our internship program.

Finding fish in new ponds works when we listen to God and choose those who are already movers and shakers in their field. Those who achieve their goals in the marketplace can easily adapt their skills and make things happen in a children's ministry.

If the first part of having the right lure is a cause and vision, the second part is keeping it measurable. Leaders want to feel that they are making a difference. There is no lure more powerful than a vision becoming a reality.

At the beginning of every year, we lay out our vision goals, and everyone gets excited. What is even more exciting is the end-of-the-year meeting when we celebrate the goals that have been reached. When our team sees that we have reached 95 percent of our goals, they see that the One who began a good work in us has completed it (see Phil. 1:6). We produce videos of lives that were impacted by our volunteers and give awards to recognize all the love, time and commitment. We usually invite new recruits to the celebration night to show them that with God's help so much can be accomplished through our gifts and talents and faithfulness.

Be Persistent!

To catch a big fish, you have to be persistent. Simon and his friends fished day and night; but it wasn't until Jesus told them to cast their nets one more time that they caught more fish than the nets could hold. A persistent fisherman who's not afraid of new ideas will catch prize fish. There are always going to be walls that seem too difficult to break through. The one thing I have always tried to be is persistent. It is that persistent determination that allows you, with God's help, to see the fruit of your labor.

Sometimes when we face obstacles, we want to go around them because it's too hard. Life is hard, work is hard and ministry can be hard. It's the persistent leaders that push through. The next time you face a brick wall, do not focus on the wall; focus on the sledgehammer. The sledgehammer is any tool that God gives us to blow a hole through the walls we face. Sometimes you will have to keep on hammering, but ultimately your breakthrough will come to pass. I learned early on to never give up on people, even if they give up on themselves. You may find yourself wanting to move on, thinking the grass is greener somewhere else. I think the grass is greener where you water it.

It felt like I was carrying the load by myself at my first job as a youth pastor. My staff included myself and a shared administrative assistant. We were busy all the time, needing to be at every event that was happening at the church. I loved the kids but we never had enough time or resources. Because we shared equipment with other ministries, I would often be running from building to building to gather music stands or microphones 30 minutes before the service. *Make sure someone is at the snack bar,* I would say to myself. *Make sure all the games are turned on and the worship team makes it. There is a drama team this week, right? Do we have any video?*

We were a production-oriented church and put on Easter productions, Christmas productions and whatever other productions we could think of. We stopped whatever we were working on to wrap Christmas lights on Christmas trees. Sometimes all we would do for two months was build sets. There was no family time during the holidays. The production was more important than the ministries for which we were hired, and most of us hated it. When events become more important than your team, it's time to evaluate what is important and what you feel is urgent. If you want to keep your team for the long haul, they can't be at every event and be asked to miss most of their family events. You lose good people when you are out of alignment.

I had such a passion to care for those kids, but I didn't want to lead like a one-man circus. I wanted to lead like a conductor in a symphony orchestra where everyone played a part. So at the beginning of my second year, I started to build people. I couldn't control the demands made by other leaders, but I could control how I led. I knew that when you build a team, they learn to lead like you. I was building relationships but had to learn how to delegate and develop people as leaders. We were just barely getting the job done, not building anything for the future.

Finally, we started building people instead of programs. We developed a parent booster club to handle fundraisers and special events. A youth internship program allowed college students the chance to speak, serve and lead teams. Our youth/parent leadership team helped with set-up and teardown. We raised money for our own equipment so it would be there when services started. Team building is a process. It costs a lot in the beginning, but it pays huge dividends in the end.

Why do so few churches operate with a team approach to ministry? No one stays long enough for the process to be completed. We work on it until the process gets too hard. When opposition comes, we tend to pack it up and accept "no" as the final answer. Timing is part of the process. It's not that your dreams won't come to pass; it's *when* they will come to pass. Be persistent. When one door closes, maybe you should look for another way into the room.

By the end of my second year, I was drained. I was at a beach day with our youth and was thinking seriously about an offer I had just received to go to another church. Right then God spoke to me, saying, "Craig, if you leave now, most of the investment you've made in others during these two years will be lost. You will have planted the seed but missed the harvest. If you stay, you will see more fruit than you can imagine; if you leave, you will always wonder what could have been." Wow! That was a wake-up call.

The process is what God is interested in, not just the end result. The process is a test of persistence, faithfulness and heart. God is more interested in building people than giving them what they want. Life is a series of tests. If you take a test and only finish half of it, it doesn't matter if you answered everything correctly. You still fail because only half of the test was completed. Being persistent means finishing what you started and purposefully fulfilling the promise.

I had a choice to quit and look for greener grass or water the grass where I was. I decided to stay, and over the next three years we experienced God's power at work in a way I'd never seen before. Multiple ministers and leaders came out of that youth department. I still have young people call me and tell me what an impact that youth group had on their life. If I had given up, I would have never seen it come to pass. Persistent determination allows you to see the fruit of your labor.

At Faith Community Church, I never let the fact that I couldn't hire more staff stop me from building a staff. I do not believe you need a large staff to grow a church. I'm not a proponent of a huge staff; I'm a proponent of high-capacity leaders. High-capacity leaders can build teams of volunteers to do what a big staff can do.

When God showed us where to fish, we ended up with Roxy and Karen, and also Therese, the architect of our new children's facility, who had never worked with children before. She ended up working on our set designs and programming. We found a world-class athlete who ended up being one of our best ministry leaders. Another diamond in the rough ended up heading up our Wednesday night program. All of them started as volunteers and went on to become as good or better leaders than most paid staff members in children's ministries across America. The money fish are out there if you know where to fish. Let's go fishin'!

Looking Up from the Trenches
Roxy Traughber
Lakewood Team Member

From a young, zealous youth pastor in Covina, California, to a leader of leaders here at Lakewood, Craig Johnson challenges his team with inspiring leadership nuggets. For me, actions always speak louder than words, and Craig has demonstrated time and time again, in word and in deed, his desire to help build people into great leaders.

Craig continually reminds his team how important relationships are in leading effectively. As we maneuver through life, it's easy to get lost in details and tasks. I've had to learn to never allow our goals to take precedence over our relationships. Craig's infamous phrase "People are our greatest assets" has become part of my vocabulary. This statement has changed my entire approach to fulfilling my purpose in life. Building people is not an option. I'm constantly reminding the people who serve with me that God has always been in the "people" business, not the "program" business. Don't get me wrong, quality church programs need to be in place to serve as tools to inspire, encourage and help meet people's needs. But all of our efforts are in vain if we fail to keep the main objective in front of us at all times: PEOPLE. After serving in ministry for over 30 years, I can honestly say that the most rewarding aspect of my life is building people.

I will be the first to admit that building authentic relationships with my ministry team does not always come easy; often it is quite time consuming. Craig has modeled the importance of building relationships with our team week after week, month after month and year after year. He encourages us to be consistent and intentional about building relationships, especially with those who are serving alongside of us. Serving at a mega church in a mega ministry with mega day-to-day responsibilities can be a mega time-management challenge. But I've seen the fruit that's produced when people are the priority. Strong, healthy relationships produce strong, healthy teams, which produce strong, healthy ministries. In my opinion, the scheduled "Investment Time" on Craig's monthly calendar is a major key to his success in developing leaders. I've learned that this type of investment pays great dividends, which fuels me to go the extra mile when it comes to making time for my team.

People are our greatest assets; however, they are still people, and people are imperfect. Failures and disappointments are simply a part of life. Sometimes we hit home runs, and sometimes we strike out. I've learned to celebrate the wins and learn from the defeats. The striking-out part is no fun—not for the team, not for the fans and especially not for the batter. But how we respond to a mistake is far more important than the mistake itself.

I understand, firsthand, how important it is to make allowances for failure when leading any team, especially your home team—that is, your family. When my daughter and I were serving in ministry with Craig several years ago, she struck out BIG TIME! She became pregnant at 16, which was a huge blow to our family and especially to Heather, who is the youngest of our three children. I'm a preacher's kid, raised in church, who went on to raise my family in church. These kinds of things didn't happen to our family. As you can imagine, my baby girl was challenged with making some very important grown-up decisions that would drastically change the course of two lives.

Our family was determined to stand shoulder to shoulder and walk through this valley together with the mindset that God is perfect; man is not. We made the no-brainer decision to support Heather throughout this entire life-changing journey. However, Heather's initial mindset was that she had put her family through the most devastating, shameful situation that we were ever going to experience in our lifetime. (She was very naïve.) Though she felt that she had failed her family, herself and her Creator, we continued to encourage her to respond with courage and take every opportunity to learn throughout the journey.

For us, looking up, focusing on who God is and who we are not was the only remedy to withstand this difficult season. We firmly believed that drawing strength and getting perspective from our Creator was our best option. Although we benefited from both professional and spiritual counseling, at the end of the day we all knew that our focus on God, gaining His perspective and drawing from His divine wisdom would ultimately be the key factor in helping our daughter make the right decisions.

It wasn't always easy for us to have a vertical perspective. Time and time again we were caught up in a confusing whirlwind of emotions, mainly because our view needed adjustment; looking out often just seemed to be more natural. After all, we wanted to move forward, so it seemed only logical to keep our eyes fixed in front of us. We needed to see where we were headed. But this caused problems with our vision, because it's impossible to keep one eye positioned vertically and the other horizontally. Were we going to trust God or not? That was the ultimate question. In the end, we stepped out in faith and moved into an unfamiliar and somewhat unpopular arena. We trusted in the fact that God knows the end from the beginning. God had a plan from the very beginning. Heather's mistake did not surprise Him; we were the ones who were caught off guard.

Without going into too many details, I can passionately inform you that it pays to keep your eyes fixed on your Creator. He is the giver of life, the great I AM. In difficult times, having the mind of God will keep us from losing our own mind. Today, both my daughter and granddaughter are full of life! They bring joy to those who are without joy. They have a positive impact on others who have been told that failures dictate one's future. Heather will be the first to tell of God's love and mercy, and His desire to turn His children's mistakes into His divine miracles.

For many months, Craig stood with our family, supporting us in prayer and encouraging us with words of wisdom. He's proven to be one of the best examples of a spiritual leader that I have ever met, not because he's perfect but because he knows he's not perfect. Craig inspires people to reach higher, move forward, dig down deep and endure hardships in order to fulfill their destiny.

QUESTIONS FOR ACTION

1. In your organization, what four qualities would define a "money fish"?

2. Identify the "over-crowded" ponds you normally fish for leaders. Consider the four qualities you want in a leader and ask God to show you new ponds in which to start fishing.

3. Consider the obstacles that have prevented you from fishing in new ponds in the past. What steps can you take to overcome these obstacles?

4. As you reflect on the story of Karen and Roxy becoming leaders, are there ways you can adapt your vision to incorporate the leaders God has placed in front of you?

5. If your team clearly stated goals for the year and then celebrated their accomplishments, what impact would that have on their attitude?

6. Would your team members describe you as a persistent fisherman who's not afraid to try new ideas? If so, how does that impact the way they view leadership? If they don't describe you that way, what would have to change in your organization if they did?

10

Become a Student of Human Behavior

Doing life is not easy. Until you learn to enjoy the process, you won't see the amazing things God is trying to teach you. Love the process; watch the progress.

I have no idea when it happened, but at some point, I took a good look at my mom and dad and realized they were totally different. My dad would be the perfect candidate for a reality show called Extreme Extrovert. As the king of object lessons, he loved to teach a life lesson at a moment of inspiration, tell stories and make you laugh. He remains the most relational person I have ever met and the ultimate giver. My mother, on the other hand, has a quiet strength. She speaks only when she has something of value to say. More introverted, my mom would make her presence known in more subtle ways. Mom was frugal, but Dad was not; and so it was Dad who bought me a brand-new Trans Am.

Having observed that my dad loved to please people, I had been talking about the car for six months, hoping my dad would find a way to make it happen. When my mom saw it, she just shook her head. She liked to plan things out, while my dad was the impulsive one.

My father was always busy doing something; my mom would pull back the reins when she'd had enough. When my dad was mad, half the neighborhood would hear it; when my mother got mad, she would just stop talking. When Mom wanted to make a point, she would give Dad the silent treatment until he bugged her enough. Then she would let him have it! You had to push my mom pretty far for her to get mad, but Dad could push her to the point of exasperation. Once, she was so mad she said, "Lloyd, you are just an old . . . old . . . jack-o-lantern." That was the worst thing she could muster up. Dad laughed, and he told that story for years. Dad was six-feet tall; mom was four-feet-eleven. Dad was a preacher, and mom was a teacher. Dad was bigger than life, a generous man who had persuasive skills that were matched by few. Mom was steady, strong and an always encouraging peacemaker. Everyone has flaws. I learned that from them too.

One of my favorite Dad stories occurred in elementary school when we stopped in Reno during a family road trip. In Reno there are slot machines in the gas stations, restaurants and even bathrooms (just kidding). As we walked into a restaurant, the lights, bells, big handles with black knobs and the displays with spinning oranges, cherries and lemons all awoke in me a desire to have just one chance to pull down that big lever. I wanted to watch all of that fruit spin while the lights flashed and the bells rang. From the minute we walked in, I was begging my dad to let me play.

"Dad, can I please play that machine with the lights and cherries, and pull the big handle?" I asked.

"No, son," my dad said, "we do not gamble, and you will just waste your money."

"But I won't waste my money, Daddy. That man over there just pulled the big handle and some money came right back to him. Please, please can I play?"

This went on all during dinner. Finally, Dad pulled out a quarter and said, "Son, I am going to teach you a lesson. Do you see this quarter? When I put this quarter into that machine, you are going to see what happens when you gamble." Then he went on, "Now, son, I want you to watch this and let it be a lesson about what gambling is all about. You never win when you gamble."

Okay, fine, I thought. *Would you please just pull back the big handle before my next birthday?*

"Okay, son, you see this quarter, this quarter is going to be gone once I put it in there."

How long can this agony last? I thought. *I just want to see the fruit spin.*

Finally, Dad put the quarter in and we pulled back the lever, and the fruit began to spin. Dad continued to remind me what a waste of time and money this was while my eyes were glued to the spinning fruit. One cherry popped up and then two. The lemon passed, the orange passed and then it seemed like time stood still as the third cherry stopped in the row. JACKPOT!

"Yes!" I yelled."

"Noooooo!" my dad cried.

Coins began to pour out of the machine at an ungodly pace. I was jumping around screaming "jackpot" and dad was trying to figure out what you do when an object lesson goes wrong. Taking the quarters, Dad was stuffing them back into the machine and pulling the lever as fast as he could, feeling that he couldn't keep the money. Unfortunately, he hit two more jackpots in the process. Exasperated and embarrassed from his object lesson gone bad, Dad took the quarters and poured them on the counter, telling the waitress, "This will probably be the biggest tip you've had all year." Turning to me, he said, "Don't say a word; just go get in the car." Dad never mentioned that experience to me again, but I never forgot it.

That was my dad: never afraid to try to make a point. Again, my mom just shook her head. They were different and yet perfect for each other. They stood by each other through thick and thin, sickness and health, till death do us part. Married for over 40 years, my father's greatest accomplishment was his marriage and family. No one loved his family more than he did. Although at the end of his life my father struggled with illness and didn't seem to be the same person, he will always be one of my heroes. My mom is still a steady rock of grace, comforting and strong. I know everything there is to know about my parents. I've learned from both of them what to do and what not to do. I've studied their lives and taken leadership lessons from them, both good and bad.

I knew how to respond to them when they were struggling and how to encourage them when they were facing an obstacle. I knew when to talk to them about issues and when not to. I knew their likes, dislikes, joys and trials. I knew what their capacity was, and I knew the potential they had within them. I knew their flaws and their talents. I learned from them that one careless mistake can cause a lifetime of hurt, but one act of grace can cause a lifetime of forgiveness. I knew just about everything you could know about two people. Why did I know them so well? I had studied them for years. I became a student of human behavior with the people closest to me. They were in my circle of influence, so I wanted to know everything I could about them to have a close family. Yet, just because you may know a lot doesn't mean you are learning anything new. Vertical leaders need to be students before they can be leaders. When the desire to learn becomes stronger than the desire to want more, you will have the wisdom to do more and it will cost you less. We need to know our teams before we can know how to lead them.

Understanding Your Team

Human behavior is influenced by culture, attitudes, emotions, values, ethics, authority and genetics.[1] We get frustrated with others when they aren't grabbing hold of the vision, but the problem may not lie in that person, but rather in our presentation. Each team member has likely come from a different background, with different influences. As we grow, we learn to follow patterns set out for us by leaders in our lives, such as parents, teachers and bosses. Some of these leaders are plodders who take their time building one brick at a time. Others may see a mountain and challenge their army to take it with them. Other leaders are process people who want to get a consensus on everything. These multiple leadership styles have had an impact on our team before they came together. Now they are a team with a new leader.

We may think it is the team's job to figure out our leadership style, but it's our job to help them understand why we do things the way we do. If the team doesn't understand the leader, it's hard for them to adapt. A vertical leader helps his team understand how to work together by understanding his leadership style and communicating why he does what he does with his team.

Understanding what makes your team tick is the next step. Once a leader can understand the individuals in the team, then they can "understand the equation" and figure out how all these different people with different backgrounds can add up to a team. Knowing yourself and knowing your team will create a team environment that is unstoppable.

I try to understand my team by asking questions not only about their areas of responsibility but also about their personal lives. I seek to understand why they do what they do. When they are frustrated, instead of quickly offering a solution to their problem, I take time to understand what it is about the situation that makes them frustrated. When I get to know them, then I can more effectively lead them.

My son is a great thinker. He does well in school; but when he gets stuck on a problem, he usually shuts down. He would love to move forward, he just doesn't know how. During his senior year,

I got an email from his math teacher saying he wasn't turning in his homework, and his last few quiz grades were *D*s and *F*s. Cory had an overall goal of getting good grades and going on to college. He was doing well in all his other classes.

I could have lectured him, telling him to go to his room and get to work. I could have told him it was his responsibility to figure things out and make it happen. Was that going to help Cory? Would that have helped him follow his vision? Instead of telling Cory it was his job to figure it out, we talked about solutions. Would a tutor help? When Cory told me the tutors at school weren't helping, we found a math teacher. After one session with a mathematician, he understood the problem. His fears were solved by the instruction of a master teacher. Relief and understanding took the place of frustration, and his grade climbed to a solid *B*. Cory graduated with a 3.8 grade-point average and was ready for college.

The Three *P*s

Just as the master mathematician needs to understand the student before she can help him, we need to understand our team so that we can help them catch the vision. We can't assume that everyone is going to know the equation. Instead we have to assume, as teachers do, that different people are at different levels at different times. Think for a moment about the good and bad teachers you have known. Teacher effectiveness has less to do with intelligence than it does with the three Ps: preparation, patience and passion.

Preparation

A good teacher or leader is prepared every time he or she leads. Let me be clear that at this point I'm not talking about being prepared with your plan of action (which is an absolute necessity), but being prepared by knowing your team so that you can communicate your vision or plan effectively. Vertical leaders know their team by name and have spent time learning what makes each student or team member tick. While it is time consuming, becoming a student of your team members before you are a teacher/leader pays huge dividends.

Patience

A well-prepared leader takes time to be sure the team understands the vision or plan before he or she moves on to the next challenge. Some of the team will learn quickly and some more slowly, but a vertical leader wants everyone on the team to succeed. A great leader does everything he can to communicate creatively so that everyone can learn and grow and meet their goals.

Remember our discussion on the tyranny of our passion? Patience, and understanding your team, effectively combat the tendency to allow your passion to run over your team members.

Passion

Vertical leaders are passionate about their team! Someone once said that good leaders are the ones you would serve with, but great leaders are the ones you personally would follow. Their passion drives them to do the little things that others are not willing to do. Teachers of the year are those who always do a little extra to help their students learn. They don't just do the job and go home. "Just doing the job" will never build great teams.

Have you lost your passion for your team because you don't feel like they are catching the vision? When I hit that wall, I return to the basics. Maybe they don't understand what it means to be passionate about something. Maybe they have lost their passion for what they do, and they need a vertical leader to help them rekindle the fire. A fire can start wherever someone lights it. When you see your team from God's perspective and you understand His vision for their lives, He will give you the matches, wood, gasoline and everything else you need to rekindle a blazing fire of passion for their lives.

Looking Up from the Trenches
Anthony Quintanilla
Lakewood Team Member

I have had the privilege of serving under the impactful leadership of Craig Johnson. I use the word "impactful" purposefully because, in my opinion, Craig has a unique ability to revolutionize church ministry by reexamining, reinventing and reimagining how ministry takes place. He constantly challenges the norm in hopes of impacting a broader range of people. With Pastor Craig, everything begins and ends with the individual.

I can remember Craig modeling the concept of being a vertical leader way before I ever heard him use the phrase "vertical leader." A few months ago, I came across a handout that I received at the first team meeting Pastor Craig conducted when he came to Lakewood Church. Craig had been at the church for not much more than a month and had laid out a plan to radically change a good children's ministry into a great children's ministry. During that meeting I am sure I was not the only person wondering who this guy was and how in the world he expected to get all this done. As I sat there reviewing that nearly five-year-old handout, I was happily amazed at how much of that dream had become a reality. At that meeting, Craig modeled vertical leadership by looking at the potential—the possibilities—and to God for direction, regardless of the situation, limitations, risks and circumstances. Since that time I have consistently seen Craig produce the fruit of a vertical leader by repeatedly being willing to risk what was good in order to have what is great.

A few weeks ago, I was in a meeting with Craig and a couple of other leaders. A month prior to this meeting, Craig had restructured the children's ministry leadership team, which resulted in my having the opportunity to take on more responsibility. Toward the end of this meeting, Craig began affirming us as leaders and emphasized that if we needed any additional support from him to let him know. At this point, Craig looked directly at me and firmly said, "Anthony, if you ever need my help, make sure you let me know. You carry things silently." In that last sentence I knew how well Craig knew me, and I knew that he had taken the time to understand me in order to better lead me and care for me. I have heard Craig tell staff members repeatedly the importance of being students of human behavior. I just had not realized the degree to which he had studied me.

One of the most important things I've learned from Craig is the art of change and the need for change. In life, everything is changing, growing or evolving. Once something becomes stagnant, decline is not far behind. Immediately upon Craig's arrival at Lakewood, he implemented dramatic change in the children's ministry and consistently implemented small changes in order to maximize effectiveness. Prior to beginning a change, Craig will prepare the ministry team. Although the exact nature of the change may not be communicated, the need for everyone to be ready for change is made clear.

The year 2009 marked a shift in ministry focus for the children's ministry at Lakewood Church. Craig felt that it was time to broaden the focus beyond just reaching, teaching and discipling the children. Now we were going to be geared toward reaching the entire family. Interestingly, Craig began preparing us for this shift at least a year beforehand by consistently directing our attention toward the needs, struggles and condition of the family. When it came time to craft a strategy to reach the family unit, the staff was prepared because of all that had been said over the previous year. Along with this shift, Craig recognized a need to elevate the overall leadership ability of the team in order to carry out the coming change. He spent well over a year systematically instilling in us essential leadership skills that would be necessary for us to successfully navigate the coming change. I'm convinced that the success we have had at Lakewood in implementing huge changes in a short period of time is due to such careful preparation!

QUESTIONS FOR ACTION

1. In the beginning of the chapter, Craig takes a long look at his parents and their relationship, modeling for us how to be a student of another person and of the relationships between people. Use the questions below to reflect on your own parents (or others close to you).

   · What makes them tick?
   · What are their personality characteristics?
   · How do they handle problems?
   · What makes them happiest?
   · What are the strong points and weak points of the relationship?

2. Consider the team members closest to you in your organization using the same questions.

3. What benefits would you experience as a leader if you took time before each meeting to prepare by taking time to understand the person you are meeting?

4. Are you naturally a patient person? How has your ability or inability to be patient impacted your effectiveness as a leader?

5. Do you have a passion for your team? Ask God to continue to develop in you a passion for the team He's placed under your leadership.

Note
1. "Culture," Wikipedia.org/wiki/Culture, accessed July 2009.

11

The Right Approach Activates the Best Response

A vertical leader never gives up on people. You may have to wait some people out, but always keep the door of redemption open and be the first one to welcome them in. Seek out the best things in the struggle, learn from it, change direction, and then encourage them to refuel and try again.

Speaker and writer Louie Giglio said, "You will accomplish more in the next two months by developing a sincere interest in two people rather than taking two years trying to get two people to develop a sincere interest in you."[1] How you relate to your team will change how they relate to you. The time you take to build them up will convince them that you care about them. Your team needs to love the person carrying the vision, not because they've invested in you but because you've invested in them.

When love and mutual respect saturate your leadership team, you've taken a giant step toward the vision God has for your success. You can't have a movement without unity. You can't have unity without trust.

Mafia Leadership Approach

One of the worst things I could have my team say about me is "I love his vision, but I can't stand him." Some leaders might say,

"Who cares if they love me as long as they do what I say and get the job done?" The motivation in that case is intimidation, or what I call the mafia leadership approach. Mafia movies are among the most watched movies in America, and while watching mafia leaders trying to balance normal family life with unscrupulous activity is intriguing, their leadership style is obviously destructive. In a mafia organization the first level are the "associates," second are the "soldiers," third are the "captains," then "underboss" and finally the "boss" who has an advisor called a *consigliere*. Interestingly, some larger churches have a similar structure! At the first level you have the "parishioners," then "volunteers," then "administrators," then "staff pastors" and finally the "pastor," with an advisor called the "executive or associate pastor."

Think for a moment about how the mafia is portrayed in most movies. Who has control, and how is it used? The boss, in total control and motivated by pride and greed, hardly ever relates to the rest of the crew unless someone has impressed him or sought him out. The lower a person's level, the less important that person is. The boss gets a piece of everything that anyone else makes. The workers don't get credit, a bonus or a promotion unless the boss gets paid. Working out of fear and control, the boss promotes fear within the entire organization. Publicly, there is a great show of affection with hugs and a kiss on the cheek, but in private there is a complete lack of trust.

In one such movie, *A Bronx Tale,* the boss is asked, "Is it better to be loved or feared?" He answers, "It's great to be both, but if I had my choice, I would rather be feared. Fear lasts longer than love." The mafia boss models fear, intimidation and power for his crew and so can never appear weak or vulnerable. At all costs, the image must be protected.

How many of us can relate to certain aspects of the mafia environment? How many of us only promote our team when it benefits us? Are we insulated from our team, only interacting with a few? Do we need to be in control of everything that happens? Do we ever lead out of fear instead of favor?

When we lead out of favor, and not fear, we realize there is room enough in our organization for the unique gifts and talents of every individual. We work to raise everyone higher, not just a select few. We don't just communicate *our* vision, but try to listen to the vision of our team members. If we really get to know our people, we'll see new ideas and fresh vision popping up all over the place. When I find out who my leaders are and what they are interested in, that is an investment of time that always pays off. At times we have created new opportunities and ministries to match the gifts and goals of the individuals.

If someone's heart is in music, I won't encourage that person to be a small-group leader, even if that is the only position we have available. I try to see if we can create a place for them within the organization. We often limit our success by trying to adjust people to our plans, rather than adjusting to the gifts and talents of the ones God sends us. If you are patient, God will bring you the right person to fit that role, as well as people to meet needs you didn't even know you had!

Jesus' Leadership Approach

Whether you've been a part of a church your whole life or you've never set foot inside any Christian organization, we can probably all agree that one of the greatest leaders to have ever lived was Jesus of Nazareth. In just three years He trained a ministry team so well that within a few decades they went from hiding in a backroom to having their organization represented in most of the major cities in the Roman Empire. His investment had long-term benefits. I'm a direct result of that investment. Now, let's be honest, Jesus and

His followers did have some pretty impressive help: the Creator of the universe. But so do you! Jesus operated on a totally different plane, and He was able to inspire His followers to extraordinary change. What was His leadership approach?

At one point, two of Jesus' friends asked Him if they could hold the first two spots on His leadership team. James and John knew that Jesus was the boss, but they wanted to be next in power. As you can imagine, the others on the team were angry and began arguing with one another. Jesus took this opportunity to teach His team to lead vertically: Leadership does not begin with the power to rule over others, but with the power to serve others. He said it this way:

> You've observed how godless rulers throw their weight around and when people get little power how quickly it goes to their heads. It's not going to be that way with you. Whoever wants to be great must become a servant. Whoever wants to be first among you must be your slave. That is what the Son of Man has done: He came to serve, not to be served—and then to give away his life in exchange for many who are held hostage (Mark 10:42-45, *THE MESSAGE*).

Jesus spent three years investing in the lives of His team. Leading out of love, not fear, He not only served them but He also modeled service to others in the way He treated everyone He met. Ultimately, He gave everything for the sake of others, and in so doing not only started a ministry but a movement that still radiates throughout the world. Because He loved them, they in turn took God's vision. And nothing has been the same ever since.

The Jesus Leadership Approach places a high priority on spending time with leaders. Jesus' team of disciples literally followed Him around the country. Investing in them, He knew their talents and their gifts. He knew Peter would make a great leader and John would be a good balance for Peter. Judas would betray Him and Thomas needed a little extra help in order to believe. Have you experienced a leader using Jesus' approach to leadership? Have you had a leader pour his or her life into you? If you have, then you know the incredible power of a leader taking time to serve his or her team so that they can more effectively serve others. If not, you can't become that leader for someone else. When you lead with this approach, people have a hard time understanding what you are doing. They think success results from the right program or curriculum. It doesn't.

It's Not About the Curriculum

Children's ministers often ask me what kind of curriculum I use. I tell them not to worry about the curriculum but to focus on who is going to be teaching it. A curriculum will only take you so far if you don't have the right team to communicate the message. Our good friends from Willow Creek came out to look at our curriculum called Extreme Kids. They wanted to see it in action, and afterwards they wanted to study it pretty thoroughly. At first I thought they didn't like what they saw and were taking a deeper look to see the flaws. Instead, they said that because they rarely see leaders so strong, they wanted to make sure it wasn't just great leaders teaching mediocre curriculum. What a compliment! I would rather have great leaders than great curriculum any day.

Don't try to make your leaders adapt to a curriculum; make sure the curriculum fits your leaders and culture. Let God show you a new way of looking at things. Quit trying to make the pieces fit and let God show you *where* the pieces of the puzzle fit. Vertical leadership is about advancing people and asking, "Am I developing a sincere interest in people or am I trying to get them to develop an interest in me?"

Trust Your Team

Why do you think people have difficulty delegating? It's not because they want to do the job themselves. And usually it's not because they're the only ones who can do it right. It's about trust. Some leaders give it away too quickly and some never give it away at all. It's just too hard; either they feel like they are giving up too much control or it's simply too difficult to invest enough time to really know if you can trust another. If you ever want to build teams successfully, you have to learn to delegate.

As a team builder, it's your responsibility to empower people to take on responsibility once you have modeled the vision. You're leading a tribe, and modeling is the key. You want to build warriors, not chiefs. If you don't model the vision effectively, someone will create their own vision, which will create new chiefs in your organization. Your job is to build warriors. As a leader, you want to have one vision with one chief and many warriors. While you have to be careful to not give it away before it's time, your job is ultimately to give away control so the vision can continue. What stops vision from moving forward? When you're still carrying responsibilities you should have given away three years ago and you're so busy getting the job done that you can't advance the vision.

When we get to know our team and understand their passions and hopes, we can begin to trust. We know that these particular people are best for the job, not because they're following our orders, but because they're fulfilling what God created them to do. It's a lot easier to delegate when you know the other person is fulfilling his or her destiny.

We didn't have teens serving in our children's ministry when I first came to Lakewood. When I asked why, I was told it could be a safety issue. Jokingly, I said, "Have you seen some of our adults?" Just because they are older doesn't mean they are any more responsible. We have to get to know others to learn about their potential. Unrealized potential is a huge waste! You can never really know someone's potential until you give that person a chance to show what he or she can do.

In Matthew 16:19, Jesus told His disciples that He was giving them the keys to the kingdom of heaven. He'd been training them for this moment, and when it came, He didn't keep the keys; He gave them away. "Whatever you lock on earth will be locked in heaven, and whatever you open on earth will be opened in heaven" (*NLT*). In other words, "I have taught you; now I am going to empower you." Imagine how the disciples felt. They had seen Jesus unlock so many doors, and now He was giving them the power to unlock doors without Him physically being there.

When you trust people enough to train them, and then you delegate responsibility, you are giving them the keys to success in their own life. "You mean we don't have to have the boss around to do great things?"

At Lakewood, we learned that God is no discriminator of age or ability or gender. I explained to our staff that if we empower these young people, they would become some of our best leaders. Five years later these teens are adults who are leading other adult leaders. Do not be limited by what you see; be motivated by what you don't see.

After our success with youth becoming great leaders, we pushed on further and began to think that kids can do some of the things that adults and teens can do. Remember what I said earlier about God directing us to fish in new ponds? I said that *everyone* has potential. We started asking why we were limiting our kids by not empowering them. We began a campaign called "Kids Taking Over the World." We had pictures of kids dressed up like doctors, firemen, businesswomen and pastors. We wanted to communicate that "if you will empower me, I can help heal people, build people, save people and feed people through the power of God." That is exactly what our kids have done. They not only serve tangibly, but they also serve spiritually.

We had a well-known church visit our campus, and they were blown away by something they saw during worship. During Lakewood's main service, we have prayer partners lined up throughout the building to pray as people are invited forward. People come in droves from all over the building. The visiting church was surprised to see that we not only had adult leaders moving into place as prayer partners, but we also had junior leaders getting ready to pray for their classmates. They were even more surprised to watch a number of our kids line up, not just to be prayed for by adults, but also to be prayed for by junior leaders. Our junior leaders had been trained in listening and prayer, and watching them care for their peers brought tears to the eyes of our visitors. We now have more than 350 kids and youth serving as part of our volunteer team.

The destiny in people can only be realized when a leader digs down deep to find their potential. Often we don't realize the potential we've been given until someone puts us in a situation that requires us to respond in a remarkable way. There is buried treasure all around us—potential buried in the lives of others. When discovered it can make a tremendous impact on the lives of others. Someone has to trust that that potential is there in order for it to be developed.

When you get to know another person, trust him or her, and empower that person, you help him or her discover his or her true identity in God. There is an incredible strength in knowing who you are and what your purpose is on earth. It's like having a GPS system in your brain feeding you a signal as God gives direction. First Corinthians 13:7 states that if you love someone, you will always believe in him or her. You will always expect the best of that person.

Looking Up from the Trenches
Kimberly Dix
Lakewood Team Member

Having worked in a different department for many years before being a part of Craig's team, I had heard about what a mover and shaker he was, but nothing prepared me for being a part of his team. My first week on the team Craig encouraged me to sit in on almost all of the meetings held in his department and visit each of the services to get to know the leaders and families. I was completely overwhelmed with the magnitude of what happened every weekend in Kidslife. When anyone asks me about the ministry, I just say that a miracle happens every weekend in Kidslife. I often think to myself, *Who in the world could have come up with a system to provide childcare and teaching for thousands of families each service and every weekend with this level of excellence?*

Yet it is not the size of the ministry but the way the ministry is carried out that is amazing. Craig leads out of love and compassion for the leaders he is called to serve and disciple. As an example, there is a young lady who started out as a first-year intern in the Kidslife ministry; I had never met anyone with so much creativity and talent. She even dressed in a bright, cheerful and creative way. Over the course of the weeks and months of her internship, a few concerns came up. Her particular situation really got my attention because in other jobs in ministry and in corporate America, I knew how similar cases had been handled, and I wondered if this situation was going to be handled the same way.

Craig had never given me a reason to think that he would not respond with compassion and love, but sometimes even as leaders we are tempted to react to things in the most expedient way. My heart sank when I thought of what might happen. However, to my relief, whenever anything was mentioned, we as a team would surround her, encourage her and pray for her. Craig would publically point out her strengths and intentionally did not focus on her weaknesses.

After the completion of her second year of internship, she had grown tremendously as she was given increased responsibilities and opportunities to learn how to identify her strengths and weaknesses and surround herself with others who were strong in her weak areas. She was totally open to the process and excelled at everything she did. Shortly afterward (with the high recommendations from Craig), she was offered two awesome jobs at great churches as a youth pastor. She interviewed and then prayed about where the Lord was leading her and accepted a position in another state. I can only imagine how she is going to impact the leaders under her, the students she serves and the families that participate in the ministry she will implement.

To me, that's vertical leadership modeled with love and compassion. I hope I can do the same; I will definitely make every effort to do so. I know that if Jesus was bodily here, and He was leading our team week after week, He would have responded the same way. Instead He chose to use and work through Craig Johnson.

QUESTIONS FOR ACTION

1. What characteristics of the Mafia Leadership Approach exist in your organization?

2. Describe the difference between the Mafia Leadership Approach and the Jesus Leadership Approach. How would you become a more effective leader using Jesus' approach?

3. In what ways has searching for the perfect curriculum or program deterred you from investing in your leadership team?

4. It's easier to delegate when you know the other person is fulfilling his or her destiny. Identify three people on your leadership team and commit to discovering their destiny. As you discover their purpose, create a place for them to put them to use in your organization.

Note
1. Louie Giglio, speech delivered in 2003.

12

The Art of Change

*In life, it's inevitable that everything changes.
The choice is whether you change your world or
your world changes you. Every day, be the
gift of extraordinary change!*

Our youth department has taken on the slogan "Life by Design." When they presented their vision, the leaders put a big blank canvas on stage and invited students to come up and put their own design on the canvas. The two things they were communicating were: (1) this is your youth group, and (2) God has a unique design for your life, but together we can put our designs on the canvas and create an amazing group. Change and creativity operate together.

When artists create a painting, they begin with a blank canvas that will change and metamorphose with every stroke of the brush. Unless the artist stops painting, the canvas is destined to become a beautiful work of art. Painting a portrait can be tedious, time-consuming and tiring work. An artist may be on a mission to finish yet be distracted and lose focus. Some changes cause artists to abandon what could have been their greatest masterpiece. Unexpected changes can do the same in our lives. Dr. Rick Kirschner says, "Change is inevitable, but progress is not."[1] How we respond to change determines what kind of progress we make. You can think about change or be intentional about change. You can't change the situation without determining what to refine.

Confronted by Change

Our family had just decided to make the big move from California to Texas, to come to Lakewood. We were leaving a place we loved to go to a place we had only heard about. My father was especially excited about our move because of his admiration for the founders of Lakewood Church, John and Dodie Osteen. Dad had watched their son Joel grow the church from 6,000 to more than 30,000 members in just a few years. My father felt that I would be blessed to be in a church that was reaching the world.

While we were making our decision to leave, I confided to my dad, "We love our church. We have so many good friends, and we are close to family. It doesn't make sense to move to Texas after only serving here for three years. We have so many good things right now." He said, "Son, these opportunities do not come around but once in a lifetime." You will never experience anything great until you see the *possibility* as greater than the *change*. I had to confess that I was so focused on the change that I was not looking at the possibilities. Change can be agonizing when you have to give up something you love for something you have yet to experience. We had no idea at that time, though, just how agonizing it would become.

We had just returned from our trip to Houston, in which we felt God's call to serve at Lakewood. My parents were ecstatic. When we told our pastors at Faith Community Church that we were leaving, it was a bittersweet moment. Their gracious and loving support made it an easier transition. Dr. Jim asked us to say our farewells to the church and staff on Father's Day weekend, and we would leave for Houston on Monday.

At two in the morning, on Friday, the eighteenth of June, I got a phone call from my mom, who was crying. "Craig? Craig?" she said. "Daddy's gone. The paramedics are working on him, but I think he's gone." My father had had a heart attack and hit the corner of the wall before he fell, and he was now lying in a pool of blood. "Lloyd, honey, stay with us, Lloyd," I heard my mom say.

"Mom, hold on," I said. "Let them work on him. It's not over yet."

"No, he's gone, Craig," my mother replied. "The paramedics have stopped, and Daddy's gone."

I jumped in the car and quickly drove to my parent's house, where I found my father still lying on the floor. Because there was blood involved, he could not be moved until the police arrived. Days earlier, my father and I were celebrating one of the biggest decisions of my life; and now, at 59, my childhood hero was gone.

Who Is in Control of Your Change?

How was I going to go to Houston now? My mind raced from one thought to the next: Mom needed me; we were still packing; my family was in shock; Dad was gone; we had to make funeral arrangements; how could I inspire others at my new job when I was reeling from grief? How much change can a person deal with at once? Unexpected change has the possibility of paralyzing us.

Change can mask itself to look like a problem when in reality it is the answer in disguise. We can't always see that the thing that might be holding us back is the very thing we have been holding on to the tightest. Change will force you to step onto the playing field when you have been comfortable in the stands. I don't know about you, but I do not live life to be comfortable; I live life to make a difference. Yet, you always have a choice: you either run from change or respond to it. You can either be afraid or affirming, passive or powerful. It all depends on whether you are handling the change or God is handling the change.

Have you ever experienced more change than you could bear? It's overwhelming . . . but it's not over! Vertical leaders don't run, they respond. They are not passive, but are powerful because they know that if they remain in Him, and His words remain in them, they can ask whatever they wish, and it will be given (see John 15:7). When things shift in life, it can be like a hurricane or a soft rain. It just depends on who is controlling the weather. Let God calm the storms in your life. His predictions are always right. At that moment, I asked God to take control of my life, to be the pilot, not the copilot.

I've never understood why people say that God is their copilot. The copilot doesn't control the plane; the pilot does. The copilot gets orders from the captain. I don't know about you, but I'm not giving God the orders when He's the One who wrote the manual. Maybe we struggle with indecision because we have taken control and made God the copilot. Remember the plane that miraculously landed on the Hudson River after an engine failure? Thank God the captain was flying the plane and had the experience to know how to glide the plane and lay it down on the water. He knew exactly how to respond to the sudden change. Sometimes you really need the captain!

A week after my father's death, we celebrated his life and buried his body. We gave our farewells to Faith Community Church on Father's day weekend, and the next day got in the car and left for Houston to work at the largest church in America. Talk about overwhelming! The only thing I knew in the midst of the chaos was that God was in control.

When you are about to start a service and nobody shows up to teach, who is in control? When your profits are on a downtrend and you don't know why, who is in control? When your marriage is falling apart and you're worried about the kids, who is in control? Either God will control the change or the change will control you.

In the midst of change, it's best to stop talking and thinking, and start listening and praying. Sometimes we need to listen instead of speak. How can we know what God is saying when we are doing all the talking? He may want to tell us what to do, and He would if we could only shut the thinking switch off and allow God to pour in His wisdom.

Our View of God Determines Our View of Change

We'd like God to be more conventional and predictable. Yet, if He were, there would be no miracles, no signs and wonders, no dreams coming to pass. There is never nothing going on with God. When you serve God, you are part of a revolution whether you want to be or not, because God is here to change the world, and you are His change agent. He's developing you so that you can grow others. God wants us to transform and emerge by understanding the possibilities that can be attained through unbridled faith. He has already written the script and is just waiting for us to fill the role.

In two weeks' time we had let go of our home, our church, our ministry and my father, and even though I knew in my heart that God was in control, my mind was guided by my insecurities instead of my faith. Letting go of something you love or you're familiar with can be very disconcerting. The more I thought about my fears and the more I expressed my uncertainties to others, the more uncertain I became. My words and thoughts were undermining my beliefs instead of my beliefs determining my words and actions. I was listening to all the reasons why I shouldn't change instead of all the reasons why I should. My faith was tested not so much by the outward circumstances (as hard as they were) but by my internal response. I was confronted by the same questions all vertical leaders face when struck by unexpected change: Did I trust God? Did I believe that going to a new opportunity, my father's death and leaving a church after three years were all part of God's ultimate purpose in my life?

One of my core beliefs is that God is constantly showing us new things, taking us new places and leading us on new paths that are far bigger than we can imagine. Change can deepen our trust in God. The decisions we make are a by-product of the change that is constantly taking place in our lives. When we have the courage to look at circumstances through a different lens, we will change for the better and make better decisions.

In the midst of my insecurities, I remembered my core beliefs and began to see God's perspective. I knew it was the right decision to go to Lakewood because of the way God had changed us and prepared us for this new transition.

What About Changes in Leadership?

When you experience an unexpected and unwanted change, you will experience a variety of emotions: shock, anger, disappointment, denial, fear and, eventually, resolve. Vertical leaders understand that it takes courage to walk through those changes. Courage is not just about facing something new; sometimes courage is about being able to let something go. When you don't want to let go, God reminds you that a new season is upon you.

Have you ever felt you could not do without a specific person in your department: What if that person were to leave? How would I replace him or her? You spend valuable time and energy worrying about replacing the one who is leaving, instead of putting that energy toward finding someone else who actually wants to be there. No one is irreplaceable besides God. The same God who brought you that person for a season will provide you with someone for the new season.

When Pastor John Osteen passed away, many wondered who could replace such a great man of faith. Yet the person who was going to take Lakewood to a whole new level was right there behind the scenes, unnoticed. But God had noticed Joel a long time ago and was just waiting for the right time.

Moving Forward with Change

As we experience change, courage sometimes entails pursuing those who are noticed the least. There may be someone on your team who has passion but doesn't flaunt it. It's not noticeable to you, but God knows the person's potential. Ask God to give you an observant eye to see those whom others overlook. The needle in the haystack or the diamond in the rough could be used to change the world. People often overlook God's choice because they allow the failures in someone's past to determine his or her future. It's easy to forget that failure can become someone's greatest asset.

Throughout the Bible, God used broken people to do great things. Abraham was a wife swapper, Moses had a speech impediment, Matthew was a thief, Peter was a liar; and yet God saw something in them that others could not see. Our mistakes become God's miracles. The leaves fall from the trees in autumn so that a new leaf can grow in the spring. Too often we hold on to the old when God wants new growth.

Focus on the Gain

Change can be fluent or it can be like dragging your fingernails across a chalkboard. Just as we need courage to let go, we also need courage to face the changes and allow God to bring new things into our lives. If your business or ministry isn't growing, maybe you have built a mechanism that fights the change process and you don't even realize it. As a leader, you not only have to have courage to change, but you also need to encourage others to change as well. Change can only be encouraged; forced changes will breed defensiveness.

Whether it is our health, our relationships, our lifestyle, our ministry or our relationship with God, there's always something that needs to change and grow in our lives. When Pastor Joel was speaking one morning about changing how we take care of our bodies, he mentioned that pork was not the healthiest thing for us to eat. My wife was sitting next to a woman who immediately shook her head and said under her breath, "Huh-uh, pastor, don't go there. You ain't taking away my ribs." My wife almost fell out of her chair laughing. Although it was funny, she noticed that the woman had a hard time getting in and out of her seat due to being overweight. One tweak in her thinking could lead to an amazing lifestyle change that would benefit her in so many ways. Yet, with change, we're usually more worried about what we are going to lose rather than what we are going to gain.

The rich young ruler in Matthew 19 faced this dilemma. He asked Jesus, "Good teacher, what must I do to inherit eternal life?" Jesus said, "Sell everything you have and give to the poor, and you will have treasure in heaven. Then come follow Me." The rich young ruler heard it and was saddened because he wasn't looking at what he was going to gain; he was focused on what he was going to lose. The rich young ruler wanted a guarantee that he had eternal life. He wanted a task that he could do to assure his own immortality. This young man missed the opportunity of a lifetime, a chance to change the world, because he focused on his riches from the past instead of the abundant riches in his future.

If you want true life transformation in your ministry, job or business, you may need to give up something you love now to be able to receive something that will take you higher later. Is it worth it to give up a certain food if you know it will give you a longer, better life? We all want comfortable change at a speed we can control. But if you want to see big positive changes in your life, you might just have to sacrifice for the bigger picture. It will cost you something.

Change Requires Patience and Balance

It's not easy to balance personal life with ministry or work. When I see people drop out of serving in our ministry, it's usually because something outside the church makes it overwhelming to serve inside the church. Everyone reacts differently when hit by change. William Bridges talks about change in his book *Managing Transitions While Making the Most of Change,* saying that "It's not the changes that do you in; it's the transitions."[2] Change is easy; transitions are hard. Change is quick; transitions are slow and messy. The art of change is delicate because people transition in different ways. The leader who moves too fast can run over some people. The leader who moves too slowly will miss the door of opportunity.

At a recent conference, I heard Pastor David Weil note three phases of transition, referencing William Bridges' book. The first phase, called "The Ending," entails all of those things (relationships, procedures, concepts) that must end or begin ending before the transition can begin. For example, when moving to a new job, you must first end the old job. Ending well helps you transition more easily into the new job. When someone leaves your ministry team, helping them leave on good terms will help the new team members have a cleaner canvas on which to paint.

The second phase of transition, "The Wilderness Journey," encompasses the barren landscape between the old way and the new way. This emotional wilderness often forges a new way of thinking. As a new team member settles in or as your team gets used to the absence of a team member, you begin to discover a new way to do things. The wilderness includes grieving the loss of what was and beginning to imagine the possibility of what could be.

When this happens you begin the third phase of a transition, "The Beginning." The beginning rarely coincides with the start of a new position. Beginnings occur when the team has accepted the reality of the change and has begun to work into the new season. It happens when people begin doing ministry the new way with the right heart and mind.[3]

Creating a Good Transition

Patience and balance are required to help others transition and adapt to change. It helps to think like a person of action and act like a person of thought. Thinking it through is wise, but the longer you wait, the harder it is to alter the situation.

We have things we know we need to change, but we allow them to lie there like a sleeping giant. Eventually, everyone will notice the giant in the room. If you have an employee or volunteer who's a great person but isn't the right person for the job, patience and balance are needed. You need a change in order for growth to happen, but you don't want to hurt someone you care about. Yet, if you don't shift this person, you will be settling for less than the best. The person could be a great leader in a different position, but he or she is not right for the current job.

Confronting the Giant

Holding on to the right person in the wrong job helps no one. The program is hurt when it has an ineffective leader, and the person is hurt when he or she is not helped to find a better fit for his or her skills and abilities. No one wins when the leader decides to linger in mediocrity instead of making a difficult decision. The only way to effectively confront a situation when you have the right person in the wrong job is to speak the truth with love. It's certainly not easy, and others won't always understand or agree with you, but ultimately it's better to be upfront than to pretend that everything is working out.

I have had to make some tough decisions with leaders I really care about who were not the right fit in our situation. Because we faced the situation honestly, they were able to find out that they were the perfect fit in another situation. Leaders are called to sometimes make tough decisions that require patience and balance. Even in the best situations, it's not easy to remove a person from leadership. If you cannot make difficult decisions, you may not be called to be a leader of leaders. A leader of leaders takes on the hard decisions that many are unwilling to set their hands to. The right choices are not always the easy choices. Leaders make the difficult decisions so that followers can walk in peace with clear direction.

Change with Dignity

You'll face times when you will need to make a change swiftly, knowing that the reaction of the person you are shifting will be negative; yet vertical leaders make sure that others are treated with as much dignity as possible. Thanking and honoring the person for the service and time they have given is important not just for their sake, but also for all the people they have invested in along the way. Even if they are not happy about the transition, when things have settled they will hopefully appreciate that you treated them with honor and dignity.

The same can be said when you transition from one job to the next. Don't put down the people who came before you; it won't make you look better. Remember, there are people who really appreciated the investment of your predecessor. Do what God has called you to do and honor those who have gone before you.

A Final Word

Vertical leaders embrace change, because God constantly creates new situations to help us grow as leaders and as human beings. As much as we might not like it, no one will remain in our lives forever. Trusting God's wisdom as people come in and out of your life, and teaching your team to do the same, will give you the vertical perspective you need to continue to paint the masterpiece He's designed you to create.

You are His masterpiece!

Looking Up from the Trenches
Debra Jackson
Lakewood Team Member

One day, Pastor Craig called me into his office and said, "Debra, you are always putting others before yourself. It's time for you to begin to dream again." That really touched my heart. He knows that I am currently taking care of my mother, but he did not know that I have been taking care of family members for more than 15 years. He just knew that I had put my dreams on hold and basically stopped dreaming. It was time for me to make some changes, which is something Pastor Craig knows is challenging!

When Craig first arrived at Lakewood Church as the children's pastor, he made some major changes to the children's programming. We had been doing things the same way for years, so the idea of change was not very popular, especially coming from the "new pastor on the block." Yet the changes have proven to be extremely successful. Our children's ministry has gone to new levels, our volunteer team has tripled, our children's attendance has more than doubled, and our children's programming is one of the best. We are in awe at how God has used one man to take the children's ministry to new heights. He makes sure we keep our programming relevant so that we can successfully minister to the kids and families of today. We continue to go from glory to glory! He is a confident leader and it shows that he is dedicated and proud of what God has called him to do. He not only leads, but he also inspires and motivates us to want to go higher!

One of the first things Craig did at Lakewood was to schedule meetings with his leaders to get to know us personally. Somewhere in our conversation, he asked me a question about how I was doing on the team. At first I did not want to respond, but I told him that I had lost my trust in some of the leaders. He gave me a firm but caring look and said, "Even when you've been hurt, you must step out of the boat and trust again. It's hard to succeed and lead others if you don't trust people. When you don't trust people, you limit yourself." Then he said, "I really need you to work on that and make a change, okay?" That statement pierced my heart. I knew God was speaking to me and saying it is time to take down the walls, make a change and begin to trust again. You might expect more from your church family, but you cannot put up walls.

We truly believe that everyone on our team is there by divine appointment. Pastor Craig has made it a point, especially in the last several years, to really seek God about who joins our team. He tries to make sure that that person is not only qualified for the position, but is also the right person and the right fit. He understands the power in unity and how much more can be accomplished when there is unity.

An advocate for strong families, Craig is passionate about families becoming a strong unit with strong faith so they can live the victorious, abundant life Jesus died to give us. He does not want any child or family left behind in wrong thinking or lack of knowledge of God's love and plan for their life. This is a big task for any man, church staff or team, but we are seeing breakthroughs in the lives of families. We have a long way to go, but we are on our way and seeing lives being changed for the better. It is a great reminder to me to never stop encouraging my children, grandchildren, brothers, sisters, aunts, uncles, and to do what I can to stay connected to my family.

Whenever I get the opportunity to share what goes on in Kidslife with another ministry or a visiting church, I am astounded at how much information I can share and how much we actually do here, and the resources that are available to us. When Pastor Craig arrived at Lakewood five years ago, he came with excellence, excitement, creativity, innovation, determination, confidence and with great purpose. God has given him the ability to see and recognize gifts and talents in others, and he's sensitive to their needs and feelings. He said to our team, "Give people what they need, not what they don't need." That really stayed with me. I don't get excited about "babying" people (or dealing with high-maintenance people), but I will do what I can for a season to help and encourage an individual move forward. Making necessary changes and giving people what they need is the right thing to do.

QUESTIONS FOR ACTION

1. What images or experiences do you think about when you read the phrase "Change is inevitable, but progress is not"?

2. Who's in control of your life? What difference does it make to think of God as the pilot and not the copilot?

3. Reflect on an experience when you allowed the change to control your decision instead of trusting that God was controlling the change.

4. Are there areas in your life at home or at work that you would like to change? Make a list of everything you will gain if that change were to take place.

5. Are there people around you that God may want to use as a leader, but you've not considered them because of past failures? Ask God to give you eyes to see His perspective and what He might want to do with the past failures.

6. Consider a recent change in your life or on the team you lead. What happened during the three phases of transition? What did you learn?

7. When faced with letting someone who is in the wrong position go, what makes it difficult for you to confront the problem? How will patience, balance and treating the person with dignity help you make the change?

Notes

1. Dr. Rick Kirschner, "The Art of Change: Skills for Life," 2009. http://theartofchange.com.
2. William Bridges, *Managing Transitions While Making the Most of Change* (New York: Da Capo Press, 2009), p. 3.
3. David Wiel, *The Three Phases of Transition,* Willow Creek Conspire Conference, March 19, 2009.

13

Commitment Levels Are Gauged by Fulfillment Levels

*Success is how others view you;
fulfillment is how you view yourself.*

When asked about my two favorite restaurants, you'll never hear me talk about fancy places with big menus and big prices. I will always choose two of the greatest fast-food restaurants to ever have a drive-thru. I know the phrase "greatest fast-food" might sound like an oxymoron, but these eateries serve great food with great service at great prices for an unforgettable experience. Don't get me wrong, they're not the only places that serve burgers and chicken, but they are among the few places that do it so well.

When I go back to California, once I get off the plane, I immediately head to the closest In-N-Out for a burger. The menu includes few choices: it's just cheeseburgers, fries and drinks. But, oh are they good! I get my double-double with fresh-cut potato fries and a chocolate shake, and I know I am home. They don't have chicken, pork, tacos or spaghetti. Their reputation rests solely on their burgers. "In-N-Out, that's what a hamburger is all about!"

Chick-fil-A is my other favorite. If it doesn't have chicken in it, they don't serve it. The best chicken nuggets, waffle fries and shakes you'll ever find. Their slogan: "Eat Mor Chikin," with a cow holding up the sign. Ingenious! I am committed to going to these places every chance I get. When I want chicken, the first place I go is Chick-fil-A. When I'm in California, the first place I go for a burger is In-N-Out.

Based on foot traffic, repeat buyers and number of stores, these two chains are two of the most successful franchises in the world. What do they have in common? For one thing, they both have hyphens in the middle of their names. Second, they were both started by Christians who established their restaurants using godly principles. Third, they have both chosen a pared-down menu, and they do it amazingly well. You won't find Chicken at In-N-Out and you won't find hamburgers at Chick-fil-A. They both train their teams well and pay them better than the rest of the fast-food industry. Their workers feel valued and they consistently offer great service. Finally, both chains make great food. People literally crave their hamburgers and chicken.

Comedian Tim Hawkins actually wrote a song about Chick-fil-A to the tune of the Beatle's song "Yesterday." It goes like this:

Chick-fil-A, I could eat there seven times a day,
Where the people laugh and children play
Oh, I'm in love with Chick-fil-A.
Suddenly, I need waffle fries in front of me,
with some nuggets and a large sweet tea,
Oh, Chick-fil-A you set me free.[1]

What makes people so passionate about these fast-food establishments? What makes people want to go back time and again? Their commitment levels are high because their fulfillment levels are high. We often think people commit themselves to what's bigger and better, but in reality people commit to quality: to what brings them the most fulfillment. These two establishments do a few things well. They established primary values and have never detoured from them. Great food, great people, great service at a great price makes for an unforgettable experience. The employees find a fulfilling place to work and the customers experience a phenomenal meal, so their commitment level shoots through the roof.

Success is how others view you, while fulfillment is how you view yourself. As a leader, others will give you lots of ideas for how to build your company or ministry. While someone else's success may inspire you, it can also have a negative impact on how you view yourself. Have you ever gone to a conference hoping for inspiration only to leave feeling overwhelmed and a little depressed? We feel like we need to become somebody else or embrace someone else's vision in order to be successful. You will never find fulfillment if you're constantly seeking after someone else's success. What has God already placed inside you? What do you do well? As a leader, have you gotten away from what you do well? You might be asking, "What do you mean, Craig?" Let me give you an example.

Commitment deepens when people feel valued. Why do you have so many ministries at your church—more than you can possibly resource adequately? Someone suggested that there was a need or maybe your team thought it was a good idea, or perhaps it is the latest trend. What happens when you start things that your budget or manpower cannot sustain for long? Ultimately you will devalue the overall program and the people that work on your teams. They don't get the support they need or they are overextended, volunteering for too many things at once. Why do we so often start programs that are outside the central vision of our church? Why do churches and businesses try to be a smorgasbord instead of an original? Chick-fil-A and In-N-Out sell hamburgers and chicken. Their vision is clear and they have stayed true to their original vision.

Too many businesses cease to be an original in an effort to fill every need a customer might have. Churches and ministries can make the same mistake. Maybe your church is meant to have a great children's ministry, not a great singles ministry. It may sound radical, but if someone came to you as a pastor and said, "We need to start a great singles ministry here at the church," you could say, "That is not what God has called us to do but the church down the street has an amazing singles program."

As churches, too often we think that if people want it, we should do it. I have seen too many people feel devalued when we started something that we should have let someone else do, because we were afraid of losing people. When Christ talks about the church, He is not talking about an individual church, but the over-all church.

Why do we do a hundred things with limited resources instead of focusing on the big goals the church or business is valued for? If the big goals are great food and great service at a great price, then stay with that and pour all your energy into those goals. Don't hold on to a ministry because someone from 1982 said it was a good idea; make sure it fits under the current vision of your church or company. Do a few things well instead of doing all of the things someone else thinks you should do. Keep it simple.

What your leader values will affect how your ministry is valued. In-N-Out and Chick-fil-A have similar value systems. If you worked for either one and struggled to provide a clean restaurant, fresh food or good service, you probably wouldn't last long. Both chains affirm that Christian beliefs and values were a foundational part of how their companies began and how they have been run over the years. Chick-fil-A's statement of corporate purpose says that the business exists "to glorify God by being a faithful steward of all that is entrusted to us and to have a positive influence on all who come in contact with Chick-fil-A." S. Truett Cathy, the founder of Chick-fil-A, says, "Our decision to close on Sunday is our way of honoring God and directing our attention to things more important than our business. If it took seven days to make a living with a restaurant, then we needed to be in some other line of work. Through the years, I have never wavered from that position."[2] With $3.5 billion in sales per year, it seems to be working out okay.

In-N-Out has been a little more subtle, printing references to Bible verses on their paper products. The print is small, containing the book, chapter and verse numbers, not the actual text. If you order a double-double, you might find "Nahum 1:7" printed on the wrapper.

If you disagree with the primary values and wanted to take one of these two companies in a different direction, you might have a problem. Let's say you wanted to serve falafels at In-N-Out or tacos at Chick-fil-A; you might have a problem getting that idea promoted.

Yet, as leaders, we sometimes allow ourselves to get taken off track and find ourselves surprised that the team doesn't want to serve tacos. When I came to Lakewood, the first thing I did was find out what was important to the lead pastor. Strong worship was important, so we built a strong music program within Kidslife. We knew we had to intertwine a message of hope and love within our program because that was a central message coming from our pastor, and it was what the church was all about. I tied what we did into what was already valued, and we got promoted because we pursued excellence in areas that were in line with our leader's heart.

If you work under a lead pastor or a company president, let me give you a word of advice: If the pastor or president is not behind what you're doing, then it will usually not get promoted. You can start a new project and run it like a grass-roots campaign, but even though it might be valuable to you, it will be a struggle to see it valued throughout your church or business. If you feel that the overall direction of the church or business needs to change, make sure you first get the leadership on board before you start implementing the change. You might ask why the pastor doesn't value what you're doing. The right time to ask that question is not two years into a program, but before you start.

Before I came to Lakewood, I asked Pastor Joel about how much he valued kids and families and what resources he was willing to put behind it. I knew that whatever he valued would be supported, and my team and volunteers would feel valued. I see a lot of frustrated leaders struggling with not being valued. It usually has nothing to do with them personally, but their projects don't reflect the passion and focus of the overall leader. Perhaps you think things should be "fair," and every ministry or department should get the same focus and support. But let me ask you a question: Do you give everything that you are doing in your life the same focus? In my life there are things that I am passionate about and there are things that I value less, based on who God has shaped me to be. One thing is not better than another, but God has made me an individual who is more enthusiastic about one area and less enthusiastic about the other. The same thing is true of your leaders. Find out in the beginning what they are passionate about and align yourself and your program to fit their values and vision. Knowing who you are, why you are doing things and who your leadership is will help you understand how to effectively build your team in the culture you are a part of.

If you want to see fulfillment and commitment levels rise, there are four questions you need to ask yourself.

Are You Clear?

Identity, identity, identity! No one wants to follow someone who doesn't know who they are and where they are going. Projecting a clear and consistent vision helps your team understand where you are going and how you'll get to your destination. The more you help your team understand consistently where you are going, and why and how you are going to get there, the better your chances of arrival. Try not to be like an advertiser, promoting the product but leaving out the small print. If you leave out the small print, people will feel that they've been misled. In-N-Out's vision was clear and simple so people could understand and follow from the beginning. "Give customers the freshest, highest quality foods you can buy and provide them with friendly service in a sparkling clean environment."[3] It was clear, simple and identifiable, and still is 60 years later. When you are clear about who you are, have an easy-to-follow vision, pursue excellence, care about your people and back up what you say, you'll build an enthusiastic group of volunteers or employees. Your ministry will have a long-lasting impact that people will still be talking about more than 60 years later.

Are You Measurable?

Have you ever been on a hot-air-balloon ride? Sometimes the ride consists of rising up into the atmosphere, floating around for a while and enjoying the view. It was more about an experience than a trip to a destination. But there are other balloon rides taken by explorers who have a crowd watching at the starting point and tracking their progress. Excitement grows as the explorer nears the destination. When they finally arrive, a crowd has again gathered to celebrate the accomplishment. Whether you were in the balloon or simply watching from the ground, you feel like you've been a part of a grand adventure.

Leading people is a lot like hot-air-balloon rides. Some leaders take their teams up in the air to float and have a good, exciting time; but when they come down, they find out they didn't really go anywhere. Other leaders map out a plan, present the goals and destination, take off for the adventure, perhaps struggle along the way but then finally reach their destination with a crowd ready to celebrate the accomplishment. In this scenario, even if you weren't a part of the execution, as you watched from afar you felt like you were part of the success.

Is it a big surprise to realize that people feel more fulfilled and their commitment level goes up when they feel like they have started and completed something? Everyone loves the excitement of starting a race *and* the exhilaration of crossing the finish line. Every year we announce our ministry goals to our entire leadership team. We tell them where we are going, how we are going to get there and we ask God to help us reach our goals. The best part of my year occurs at our celebration team meeting when we share the things God has helped us accomplish. I get excited as I watch the faces of individuals that began the race with great expectation and ended with a victory. Joy fills the room. Fulfillment levels reach an all-time high at the end of the year and produce high commitment levels for serving in the year to come.

This isn't just important for the ministry, but it's also important for the individuals we are trying to build. Our desire at Lakewood is that we build into the professional and personal lives of all our volunteers. Some have struggled and have never been taught how to finish something they've started. They've never experienced the fulfillment that comes from a job well done. One of the most valuable leadership lessons one can learn is how to finish something well. When our leaders learn to set goals and measure their success in their ministry, they often take those tools into their homes and work places. Remember, vertical leaders don't just care about how the person works in the organization; they care about the individual's personal life and growth as well.

Are You Easy to Follow?

Why do people, in record numbers, follow Joel Osteen rather than other people? Joel, like many leaders, has a solid spiritual life and a deep love for others. He genuinely wants to see people discover God's best. While those characteristics are foundational, one of the biggest reasons people listen to Joel is that he is easy to follow. He teaches and expresses himself with great clarity. I'm always taken aback when I ask a leader about their business or ministry and I get a complicated response about the intricacy and depth of their work. I think to myself, *Will the average person really understand what they're talking about?*

Kidslife operates five different services, with one in Spanish, and has 1,350 volunteers working with different teams. Our leadership structure includes staff, service leaders, ministry leaders, teachers, helpers, programmers, worship teams, bands, drama teams, special-needs professionals, and so on. Sometimes I wonder how this program ever gets done and how God makes it work every week. If I think about it too long, I get overwhelmed and my head begins to spin. Why does it work? We have a simple and clear purpose: We build people. Each leader's primary goal is to build and inspire their people. God builds and inspires us, so we build and inspire others. It's easy to follow, not too complicated.

Chick-fil-A's slogan is, "We didn't invent the chicken, just the chicken sandwich." They want to serve the best chicken, with the best service: simple and easy to follow. People love to follow something they can actually understand. When people in Houston want a good, fast chicken sandwich, they know where to go. The customers are committed because Chick-fil-A's vision is easy to follow: It's good, and they do it right. You know what they specialize in; you know what they're good at; and anywhere you go in Houston you will see the billboard with a cow holding up a sign saying, "Eat Mor Chikin." Jesus was not complicated. He said to go into the entire world and preach the gospel and make disciples: Easy to follow. Why do we complicate things?

Are You Giving People Something to Look Forward To?

There is nothing more depressing than to have nothing to look forward to. Giving people something to look forward to turns what was once unmemorable into what is now unforgettable. At Kidslife, we "premiere" everything, no matter how big or small. Making things into a big deal gives our team something to look forward to. Our big dream meetings at the beginning of the year also serve this purpose, always highlighting something new for the upcoming year. Many times it may not be a new idea but a creative reinvention.

Many years ago, we started a program called The Champions Club for special-needs kids. Because it was done within a few regular classrooms, very few people at Lakewood knew anything about it. We wanted to take the program to another level, so we reinvented it with a new philosophy of building the mind, body and soul. We added a physical therapy room, a sensory room and a spiritual therapy room. After presenting the ministry in its new package to the congregation, it is one of our more impactful and recognizable ministries. Doing this in different ways, every year we get our people talking about what is to come.

Habakkuk 2:2-3 says, "And then God answered: Write this. Write what you see. Write it out in big block letters so that it can be read on the run. The vision-message is a witness to what's coming" (*THE MESSAGE*). In other words, prepare them for what is coming. Give them something to look forward to. There are no ordinary moments. God is always doing, showing or saying something. Help your people to believe, watch and listen with great anticipation.

Looking Up from the Trenches

Luis López
Lakewood Team Member

My wife and I moved from Colombia, South America, to work with Pastor Craig. From the beginning, he told us to always inspire people and build teams. Well, when we started encouraging and inspiring others, something began to happen. When we would tell them, "You're not just a volunteer, you're a leader," they began to think and act differently.

A group of people that were discouraged are now speaking to others about the adventure of serving in ministry. Taking ownership of the ministry, they are recruiting new volunteers and serving others on a one-on-one basis. After only two years of building teams and creating a family environment, our Spanish Ministry team has grown from a team of 60 to a team of more than 300 dedicated volunteers.

Our program will never be more important than the people, as we work hard to differentiate between what is urgent and what is important. To live out our faith at home is more important than the messages we preach; to pastor the people that we already have is more important than only focusing on how we can recruit. We have been modeling the leadership skills we've learned, and while we know we have a long way to go, we can already see how lives have been changed. We invest in our team, not expecting them to repay us. Yet, because we have invested in them, we have been greatly blessed. When we face difficult situations, our team, just like a family, has shown up to help us.

My mother-in-law passed away unexpectedly this year. Of course, when my wife got the call her heart was broken. We started planning to travel to Colombia, but with no budget for tickets for all three of us, we were only able to send my wife to be with her family. To our surprise, within a few days after my wife left, a couple from our team called and offered to pay for my entire family to travel to Colombia for the funeral. This was a huge act of kindness and a direct result of how we build and invest in our team. When we returned from Colombia, our team loved on my wife like she was family. Our team here at church has become our family, as our immediate family is miles away from us.

We began to encourage one of our first-grade teachers (who is so shy that she would hardly talk to others) about the calling of God that is on her life. We wanted to stretch her and her faith and offered her a volunteer position within "Niños Con Vida," Kidslife's Spanish Ministry. I wanted to see if she would step up, and I have been amazed to see how God has worked. Today, after only eight months of working in our Spanish Teen Life program, she is one of our most dynamic leaders. In constant communication with our teens and parents, she is a huge part of why our TeenLife program has gone to another level. We are now discipling and training approximately 100 teens on a weekly basis.

Vertical leadership can change your life and help you stop thinking with the mind of leadership and start thinking with the mind of God. When we stay disciplined and keep our daily appointment with God, we stay connected to Him and receive the instruction we need to be vertical leaders.

QUESTIONS FOR ACTION

1. What restaurants/stores do you frequent regularly, and what produces your commitment?

2. In what ways has trying to live up to someone else's view of success made your job less fulfilling?

3. Has a multitude of ministries/tasks decreased the fulfillment levels of people in your organization? If so, what could you do to immediately change this situation?

4. Is your vision for the organization in alignment with the organization's visions? What impact does this have on your level of fulfillment and commitment?

5. Do your words and actions communicate clearly? What can you do over the next month to present a clear and consistent message to your team?

6. Are you measurable? With your leadership team, create steps you can take to measure and celebrate your successes.

7. Are you easy to follow? Reflect with some trusted leaders on whether you are easy to follow.

8. Are you giving people something to look forward to? With your team, consider how you create an atmosphere of expectation.

Notes

1. Tim Hawkins, "Chick-fil-A," www.timhawkins.net/video.php (accessed July 2009).
2. S. Truett Cathy, Chick-fil-A corporate homepage. http://www.chick-fil-a.com (accessed July 2009).
3. In-N-Out corporate homepage. http://www.in-n-out.com (accessed July 2009).

14

When a Team Becomes a Family

Try to love so deeply that from the time it leaves the depths of your soul and travels to the moment you say I love you, the distance would take a lifetime to cross.

I read a blog by a woman named Dr. Janice who wrote a piece called "A Family Is a Team," about a family member who had just passed away. This is what she said:

My Uncle Phil passed away late Monday night, and today was his funeral. He was around 93 or 94 as far as I can calculate. As we gathered at the cemetery, it was eerily reminiscent of a virtual team coming together for some face time. Some people see a lot of each other, some are only seen at the obligatory times of life transitions. And some stay in the shadows and are never seen. One is the subject of brief discussion. No one's heard from him in years and no one seems to miss his presence. No, I think, it's exactly like a team. You don't get to choose your relatives and, most of the time, you don't get to choose your team. You work with what you have, respect each other for who they are, and try your best to do what needs to be done.

Phil went to work every day, selling fur coats in New York City, well past his ninetieth birthday. After Jeanette, my aunt, and his life partner of over 50 years, died, age caught up with him. A leg infection finally stopped him from taking the subway from Forest Hills every day. It was at that point that I realized we had more in common than family. We were hidebound entrepreneurs that had no intention of hanging up our boots. But now he was resigned to moving in with his daughter and her husband. They took him to work with them—they run a small clothing shop—but there isn't room on a team for two who want to do the same thing. Especially when one has no industry experience and flagging energy.

So I'd call him when I was on the street in Philadelphia, walking from home to office to appointments wherever I had a few minutes. We talked about business, mostly his, since in both our minds he would soon return to it, and market intelligence would be vital to his commercial success. My inputs were limited but appreciated: things like, this was the first day it was cold enough for people to wear fur, what the Walnut Street furrier was showing in his window, what the fur protesters were saying. It was a way of staying in the game—being on the team.

Today we celebrated his place on our family team, we of rapidly declining numbers. Among the mourners was a young man I didn't remember. But I recognized his name: Phil's employer of many years, Neustadter Furs.[1]

Have you ever wondered who will attend your funeral? When you look back at your life, who is really a family member and who is virtual family? Some of Dr Janice's family members had no real connection to each other, and Phil might have been closer with his employer than his own family. Do you need to be a blood relation to be family? I have dear friends I work with who are closer than relatives that I haven't seen for years, not because anything bad has happened in our relationship but because of distance.

Recently, my grandmother Johnson passed away at 95 years of

age. Grandma Johnson was a strong, feisty woman who lost her husband when her boys were young. She worked as a nurse all day and sometimes into the evening to provide for her family. Yet, despite the fact that her family was her life, I was the only one at her funeral. She had outlived her siblings, some family members couldn't be there due to circumstances, and some had lost touch over the years and may not have even known she had died.

Standing in front of her casket with the two funeral attendants, I conducted a service with no one in attendance. Sadness crept over me as I honored my grandmother and told her how much I loved her. As I walked away from her casket, I silently asked God, "Please don't let me be the only one the minister addresses at my funeral. Let me have not just my immediate family there, but also my extended family from the places I've worked, the friends I've met and the people who have touched my life as well as those whose lives I've had the privilege to impact." At the funeral, I began to realize how important relationships are. Your life is not going to be marked by the money you make or what you accumulate. Your life will be marked by the relationships you have built.

You Can Have a Virtual Family or a Real Family

Have you ever played a virtual reality game like "Sims"? Created by game designer Will Wright, Sims is a virtual world that allows you to interact with, control and to some extent connect emotionally with a computer-generated "family." A Sims family is easier to deal with than a real one; there is no sacrifice involved, and when you get tired you can tune them out or turn them off. Sadly, I see teams that live this in the real world. They work together but don't know each other. They do their job, keeping their office doors closed until it's time to head out for lunch. I've seen volunteer teams come to serve their two hours and then fly out the door with little interaction outside of small talk. When this happens, volunteers feel like they are doing a job rather than being a valued part of a team. Bosses that have no emotional connection with their team tune them out or turn them off when they want to. They say, "It's not personal; it's just business," which is another way to say, "I care less about our relationship than about the job getting done." Without meaning to, it's easy to lead in such a way that your team becomes more a virtual family than a real family.

One of Steven Spielberg's most extravagant films, *A.I.*, tells the story of David, a twenty-second-century childlike android programmed with the ability to love. Global warming had led to a drastic reduction of the human population, and in response, new humanoid robots called "mechas" had been created who were capable of emulating human thoughts and emotions. An advanced model named David was created to resemble a human child and to virtually "feel" love for its human owners. David was tested on a couple, Monica and Henry Swinton, whose own son had been placed in suspended animation until a cure could be found for his rare disease. Monica began to warm up to David after activating his imprinting protocol, which caused David to irreversibly bond with her as a child does with his parent. David is also befriended by Teddy, a robotic teddy bear, who takes responsibility for David's wellbeing.

Together Teddy and David set out to find the Blue Fairy, whom David remembers from the story of Pinocchio. He hopes that she will transform him into a real boy, so Monica will love him as she had loved her son. When he finds that the Blue Fairy is only a statue, a disheartened David attempts to commit suicide by falling from a ledge into the ocean.

Two thousand years later, Manhattan is buried under several hundred feet of glacial ice, and humans are extinct. Mechas find David and Teddy, the only two functional robots who knew living humans. Using David's memories, the mechas reconstruct the

Swinton home and explain to him that he cannot become human. However, they can re-create Monica from a lock of her hair that has been faithfully saved by Teddy, but she will live for only a single day. David spends the happiest day of his life playing with Monica, and as she drifts off to sleep, Monica tells David that she loves him and has always loved him. After this "everlasting moment" that David had been looking for, he closed his eyes, passed away and went to "that place where dreams are born."

Although I wanted to, I could never connect to this story. Replacing a real child with a robot was disturbing. I could see all the family members trying to interact in the movie, but it never made sense. Why? You can't throw real emotions into fake environments.

Real, healthy families are about more than just occupying space; they are about living life together. Real families need encouragement, patience and quality time. It takes them to a higher plane when their needs are met. Real families support each other in their jobs as well as their personal life. If I had a problem at work or in my personal life, I could talk to my wife or my mom because I know my family would support me. Why can't we build environments for our teams that allow for courageous conversations and amazing accountability?

A real, healthy family cheers one another on and never lets competition break up the family. Real fathers want to help their sons do greater things than the fathers have done. Are we blind to the fact that on our teams we have "sons and daughters" who are there not to be lorded over but to be mentored? When you cheer them on and help them do greater things than you could have done, you will build a family tie that is unbreakable.

Real, healthy families discipline in love to help the children grow, not to tear them down. Children need to learn from their mistakes so mistakes aren't repeated. The same can happen with our teams. We need to speak the truth in love to our teams so that we can shape people like a potter shapes clay. A potter will guide the clay with his hands until it is formed into a beautiful work of art. Isaiah 64:8 says, "Yet, Oh LORD, you are our father. We are the clay, you are the potter; we are all the work of your hand."

In a healthy family, the family members are willing to lay down their life, goals and desires for the sake of each other. When your team feels that you would lay things down so they can be encouraged and lifted up, you will have a tremendous culture change. I would give my life for my kids. I believe, without hesitation, that I would give my life for my friends and family. Love is all about sacrifice. John 15:13 says, "Greater love has no one than this, that he lay down his life for his friends." Would you give your life for the sake of your team? We are talking about a depth to which most teams never go. This is where a team becomes a family. Would I sacrifice for my team so that they could rise higher, or give up something important to me so that someone on my team could be lifted up? The answer is yes. We have lived life together and they know me, and I know them. They know that I will be there for them, and they will be there for me because we have lived it out.

When Hurricane Ike hit, our staff was spread out all over Houston. We used walkie talkies and cell phones to call our team every two to four hours to make sure they were okay. Staff members opened their homes to other staff members. If we were unable to contact a team member by phone, we sent a team member who lived nearby to check on them. The storm caused a lot of damage to some team members' homes—roofs blown off, flooding and power outages that lasted two weeks. We sent out teams to pump the water out of our team members' homes and bring food and ice. We rebuilt fences and cleared yards and driveways. Why did we do all that? Because we were not just a team; we were family. Our team members absolutely see each other in a different light now!

Loyalty grows when you become a family. Passion grows when you become a family. Humility grows when you become a family. Trust grows when you become a family. Love for one another grows when a team becomes a family. For a team to become a family, faith is essential, unity is key, sacrifice is fundamental, humility is inherent and love is the catalyst.

Your Sacrifice Will Become Their Inheritance

There is no return on an investment without sacrifice. Your team is your greatest asset. What kind of return you get depends on how, as well as how much, you invest in your team. Quantity is not always quality. What we need to sacrifice will be different in every situation. God may test us to see what we are willing to give up so that He may fill us. What you pour out allows space for what God wants to pour in. The more you give away the less baggage you carry as you move forward. John 3:16 says, "For God so loved the world that he gave his only Son, so that everyone who believes in him will not perish but have eternal life" (*NLT*). His sacrifice became our inheritance.

If you as a leader want people to follow you, trust you, believe in you and receive you, it will flow from how you give to them. The deeper you love someone, the more you want to give. If you do not like your team, there's a good chance they won't like you. If you love your team like a parent loves his or her children, you will pour into them in ways you wouldn't have if you just liked them. We know that our leaders care about us not just by what they tell us, but also by how they invest in us.

The Greatest Gift

I'm reluctant to tell this story because I know this is something that Joel and Victoria would rather keep private. The Osteens are who they are and where they are because of things others never see. When God speaks to them, they sacrifice what they have in order to invest in others. They always give their best.

My wife, Sam, and I had just received the news that our son Connor was autistic and would need help developmentally. We began to look into what it would take to give him the best medical, nutritional and developmental care we possibly could. Although I am paid a good salary, his needs were beyond what we could afford with our other family obligations. Some of the recommended treatments were astronomically expensive. My wife would wait until I got home and then hand me the papers with projected costs. I reassured her, telling her we would do whatever it takes, even if it meant selling the house or our cars.

Every night, though, I would hear Sam upstairs crying by Connor's bed after she put him to sleep, saying, "Please, God, make a way to help our son so we don't have to sell our home." She didn't know I was listening, but I could hear every word through the baby monitor in our bedroom. I would walk up the stairs and peek into Connor's room, and there Sam would be, sitting next to his bed praying to her Father God.

I had told immediate family, but few others. It was the week of summer camp, and I was getting ready to head to the church to send the kids and the team off for camp. But first I had to find our realtor's phone number to let him know we needed to sell the house. Oddly enough, I couldn't find the number and had to head to church without it. While we were getting the kids ready to leave, I received an unusual phone call from our business administrator. After asking how I was doing, he asked about Connor, which really surprised me, as I had assumed he was calling to discuss my budget. I will never forget what he said next. "Hey, Craig, I just talked to Joel, and we don't want you to have to worry about Connor's schooling or medical bills. We want Connor to have the best schooling and medical help, so Joel wanted me to tell you that it is taken care of." Tears began to stream down my cheeks as I thought about my wife sitting next to Connor every night, asking God for a miracle. I thanked Kevin over and over again, crying over the phone as I realized that God had just showed up.

When I called Sam, she began to weep, saying, "Thank You, Jesus," over and over. What kind of people do this? Who allows himself or herself to be used by God to this degree? Not employees, not bosses, but family. Regular teams would never give a gift so great that it would change someone's life forever, but Joel and Victoria Osteen, Dr. Paul and Jennifer Osteen, Kevin and Lisa Comas, and Marcos and Mariam Witt are not just people on the Lakewood executive team; they are my family.

Outside of my relationship with Jesus Christ, and the gift of my wife, kids and family, that is the single greatest gift we have received in our lives. I would go to the ends of the earth for our family at Lakewood. I would go into a burning building to save any one of them, because they helped save us. They didn't have to do that. It wasn't their obligation. Yet that's what happens when a team becomes a family. The family becomes the gift. It wasn't the size of the gift; it was the response of the giver.

What effect does it have on people when they know they are not just team members, but family? They will go to the ends of the earth for you as a leader. They will cheer you on at every turn; they will stand by you when others would leave.

Vertical leadership is about building people, not things. When you die, nothing you ever owned will matter, but everything you ever did will. I find that when I am overwhelmed by God's love, it's usually when I have just given His love away to someone else. When I give a little, He gives me much. When you become a vertical leader and your team becomes a family, it is a new day. What the previous day brought cannot compare to what this day will bring. Embrace it; believe that today is no ordinary day. There will be a day to walk into the sunset if you allow God's light to shine on the road that leads to it.

Your best days are out in front of you. Keep dreaming big!

Looking Up from the Trenches
Candice Davis
Lakewood Team Member

I grew up in a small church in Indiana, and have served in children's ministry since I was 11 years old. When my husband's job transferred us to Texas, and we began to attend Lakewood, I was definitely not getting involved in the children's ministry. I was burned out, and so together my husband and I got plugged into a marriage class. And that is where we met Pastor Craig Johnson. For some odd reason, after class he came up to me and told me that he wanted to talk to me about children's ministry. I agreed politely, but I already knew I wasn't going to contact him. I was done with children's ministry.

The next week it was announced that Pastor Craig and his wife would not be in our marriage class anymore. I was off the hook! Yet, four months later, my husband went to drop our kids off at the kids' ministry while I waited for him in the sanctuary. He came back saying that he had seen Pastor Craig, who said he still wanted to talk to me. We had only met him once. I knew it was God. When Pastor Craig caught up with me later, he told me that it was God, and that he had a project for me in the children's ministry. I became the volunteer Assistant Extreme Kids Director, and Pastor Craig began pouring into my life as a leader. I learned how to lay out vision, to recruit, to build teams and watch a vision unfold. Several months later, I left my teaching job to work at the church.

Sometimes when I hear Pastor Craig's ideas, I think, *Man, where did he come up with that?* He constantly challenges his team to go higher and dream bigger. Several years ago, Craig wanted to start a junior leaders program. I felt led to help and told Pastor Craig that I would *help* assist whoever was in charge. When the woman that was in charge resigned, he called me in to ask if I would take charge of the whole program. I was *terrified*. I wasn't ready. I didn't want to—not because I didn't want to but because I didn't have enough confidence in myself. Craig encouraged me, helped me realize that I could do it and walked me through the process, and we were on our way.

After months of planning, it was time for the kick-off party. Let's just say that it didn't go as well as I had planned. That night I learned yet another lesson. Pastor Craig remained positive, despite all the negatives. He spoke into my life and said, "This is going to be bigger than you could dream—so dream bigger." That stayed with me for a long time.

As leaders, we should always be positive and dream big. When we had a debriefing meeting later, he shared some things with me that we could definitely improve. This too was a lesson learned. When approaching your team, timing and delivery is everything.

Pastor Craig truly loves his team as family. He has proved this to me in many ways, but there are two that really stand out. One happened during Hurricane Ike. Being from the Midwest, we were new to hurricanes. We were all sent home to begin preparing for the hurricane that was coming. During the hurricane, Pastor Craig's leadership really stood out. He called us several times to check on us all. He set up teams to visit several staff members to make sure they were all right. He treated us all like we were his family, leading us during this time like Jesus leads. He was taking care of his staff as Jesus took care of His sheep.

Recently, I was going through some serious family issues, and Craig called me every day for two weeks. His words of encouragement and his love during that time spoke volumes to me. He did not have to take the time to call just to see how I was doing. During that time, Pastor Craig was more than a leader to me; he was a role model, a friend and a father figure.

QUESTIONS FOR ACTION

1. What thoughts come to mind when you read, "Your life will be marked by the relationships you build"?

2. What benefits would your team experience if they saw building relationships with each other as a core value of success?

3. What keeps most leaders from building environments for their teams that allow for courageous conversation and amazing accountability?

4. Of the characteristics of a real, healthy family in this chapter, which does your team possess and which do they lack?

5. What impact would an attitude of sacrifice for one another have on the development of your team as a family?

6. Does your team know that you like them? Love them? What can you do to demonstrate your commitment to your team?

7. Create a plan to develop a sense of family with your team. Implement your plan over the next six months and record how your organization develops.

Note
1. Dr. Janice Presser, "Ask Dr. Janice 2009." http://www.drjanice.wordpress.com (accessed July 2009).

ACKNOWLEDGMENTS

Thank you to my best friend and heavenly Father, Jesus Christ.

Thank you to Sami, Cory, Courtney and Connor. You are my love and human sunshine.

Thank you to Pastor Joel and Victoria, the ultimate vertical leaders.

Thank you to my partners in the book, Tom Stephen and Ginny Starkey.

Thank you to Bill Greig, III; Bill Denzel; Kim Bangs; Alex Field and the entire Regal family.

Thank you to our dear friends and partners in ministry, Clayton and Ashlee Hurst, and my armor bearer, Debra Jackson, and the entire Kidslife family. We have experienced when a team becomes a family.

Thank you to Dr Paul and Jennifer Osteen, for modeling grace to me in every way.

Thank you to our matriarch Dodie Osteen, and to Kevin and Lisa Comas, Marcos Witt, Duncan Dodds, Todd Fisher, Don and Jackelyn Iloff, Barbara Curtis, Randall Gonzalez, Steve Austin, Brian Tankersley, Jon Swearingen, Reed Hall, Jason Madding, Regan VanSteenis, Nick and Summer Nilson, Roxy Traughber, Steve and Tammy Crawford, Mark and DeDra Greathouse, Marcus and Cindy Ratcliff, Israel and Meleasa Houghton, Dr. Jim and Marguerite Reeve, Dan and Amy Reeve, Kim Dix, Dawn Smith, Karen Watkins, Alice Bell Gaines, Michael and Fiona Mellet, Stephanie Lloyd, Ali Templer, Tony and Kathy Salerno, Kuk and Stevie Harrell, Bob and Sherry Reeve, John and LeAnn Johnson, Norman and Etta June Surratt, Dwight and Tricia Surratt, Wendell and Lynda Vinson, and Doyle and Dolores Ferguson. You all have been vertical leaders in some way in my life. Thank you!

Thank you to all the contributors who gave their testimonies in the book. You know who you are . . . you're in the book!

To my dear mom, Carol (I love you, Mom); Chris, my bro from another mo' (ha!); and Radonda, my sister, I love you more than you will ever know. Thank you to Justin and Julie, Grandpa and Grandma Surratt, Grandma Johnson, Grandpa Floyd and Karyn Kopp, Lisa and Kevin Wright, Matt Baker, Brett and Laurie Stoneroad, Chad and Andie Allred, and to my father, Lloyd, who before he died dreamed of writing a book but never had the opportunity to do so. Here is your book, Dad.

Thank you to the entire Lakewood staff and congregation. You make it happen every week! You are amazing!

Finally, thank you to every volunteer, staff person and leader I have had the honor and privilege to work with in my lifetime. The honor was mine. Remember, when you build others, God will build you!

Ministry Contact Information
Conferences, Seminars and Retreats

Craig has been a leader of leaders as a church planter, executive pastor and director of kids, youth and young adults in his 20-plus years of ministry. He understands the challenges that leaders face in recruiting and building teams. His experience in leading multiple facets of ministry and leadership can help your church or business grow to the next level. If you would like Craig to come and speak or lead a training seminar for your group, please send an email to **leadvertically@orbitmedia.tv** or contact Orbit Media Group at (615) 550-1726.

You can follow Craig's posts on the Lakewood Facebook fan page and the Lakewood Church twitter account and check out periodic blog posts from Craig at **www.lakewood.cc.** Also, visit the following:

For Lakewood Church resources:
www.lakewood.cc

For Joel Osteen resources:
www.JoelOsteen.com

For Victoria Osteen resources:
www.VictoriaOsteen.com

Check out the new *Lead Vertically* leadership DVD resource, releasing soon as part of the CM Connect Leadership series. Also coming soon is an exciting new curriculum for churches, kids and families from Craig Johnson, Lakewood Church and KIDMO.

More Great Resources from
Regal Books

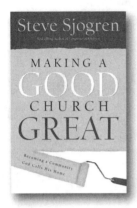

Making a Good Church Great
Becoming a Community God Calls His Home
Steve Sjogren
ISBN 978.08307.46620
ISBN 08307.46625

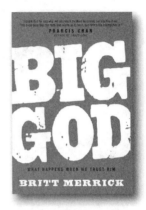

Big God
What Happens When We Trust Him
Britt Merrick
ISBN 978.08307.52225
ISBN 08307.52226

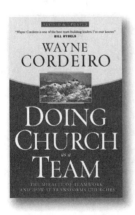

Doing Church as a Team
The Miracle of Teamwork and How
It Transforms Churches
Wayne Cordeiro
ISBN 978.08307.36812
ISBN 08307.36816

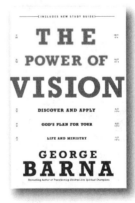

The Power of Vision
Discover and Apply God's Vision
for Your Life and Ministry
George Barna
ISBN 978.08307.47283
ISBN 08307.47281

Regal
God's Word for Your World™

Available at Bookstores Everywhere!   www.regalbooks.com